Growing
Language
& Literacy

Growing
Language
& Literacy

grades
K–8

STRATEGIES FOR ENGLISH LEARNERS

Andrea Honigsfeld

HEINEMANN
Portsmouth, NH

Heinemann
361 Hanover Street
Portsmouth, NH 03801–3912
www.heinemann.com

Offices and agents throughout the world

The author and publisher wish to thank those who have generously given permission to reprint borrowed material:

Figure 2.14: Photo by Carol Salva. Used with permission from the San Felipe de Austin State Historic Site, Texas.

Figure 3.16: Presentation Planning Guide adapted from the student handout by John Larmer, Buck Institute for Education, Novato, CA. www.pblworks.org. Used with permission.

Acknowledgments for borrowed material continue on page xx.

Library of Congress Cataloging-in-Publication Data
Names: Honigsfeld, Andrea, author.
Title: Growing language and literacy : strategies for English learners / Andrea Honigsfeld.
Description: Portsmouth, NH : Heinemann Publishing, 2019. | Includes bibliographical references.
Identifiers: LCCN 2018056934 | ISBN 9780325099170
Subjects: LCSH: English language—Study and teaching—Foreign speakers. | Literacy—Evaluation.
Classification: LCC PE1128.A2 H587 2019 | DDC 428.0071—dc23
LC record available at https://lccn.loc.gov/2018056934

Editor: Holly Kim Price
Production Editor: Sonja S. Chapman
Typesetter: Kim Arney
Cover and interior designs: Vita Lane
Cover Image: © PhotoAlto/Sandro Di Carlo Darsa/Getty Images
Manufacturing: Steve Bernier

Printed in the United States of America on acid-free paper
23   22   21   20   19   CG   1   2   3   4   5

I dedicate this book to all the children who have come to this country with their hopes and aspirations and to their brave families who left everything behind to find a better life.

I also dedicate this book to my children, Ben, Jacob, and Noah. I have loved the wonderful years of watching them grow their languages and literacies.

Contents

CHAPTER TWO

Supporting EMERGING Level English Learners

CHAPTER FIVE

Supporting BRIDGING Level English Learners

Acknowledgments

This book would not have been possible without the participation of many educators from around the United States. I acknowledge your generosity, professionalism, and commitment to helping me relay the story of our students *who really can*! Your contributions to case study vignettes are most appreciated. I appreciate how you took the time to tell me about your students you so passionately support, as well as to share your own success stories, instructional materials, photographs from your classrooms, and your students' work contributing to the rich illustrations in each chapter: Bethel Aster, Jill Ayabei, Harry Baumander, Jessica Black, Ashley Blackley, Courtney Braese, Caroline A. Brokaw, Andrea Calabrese, Michelle Castor, Allyson Caudill, Nancy Cerbone, Rosalie Cervini, Kayla Cook, Kelley Cordeiro, John Cox, Jaslyn Davies, Jennifer Watters Delahunt, Michelle D'Errico, Marisa DeSerio, Rich D'Esposito, Elena Dokshansky, Jessica Dribnak, Maryann Lo Duca-Peik, Amy Eckelmann, Nikole R. M. Emerson, Christine Engelhardt, Nicole Fernandez, Astrid Emily Francis, Laura Fuentes, Kimberly Fuller, Mike Gargulio, Michelle Gill, Jennifer Gingerich, Yara Graupera, Lisa Greenwald, Ruth Goldstein-Hernandez, Valentina Gonzalez, Molly Haag, Rob Hillhouse, Gregory Hines, Jamie Hoesing, Carlota Holder, Victor Honigsfeld, Jessica Houston, Alejandra M. Howell, Cydnie Jorgenson, Alexandra Kavouras, Sara Knigge, Mariola Krol, Katherine Lameras, Mary Langon, Sandra Larsen, Kim Lastig, Claudia Leon, Laura Leonard, Suzanne Malcuit, Samantha Mallahy, Nicole Marino, Simone Marques, Tracy Martin, Dana Moccio, Hillary Moss, Rupali Nagpal, Kelira Osca, Adriana Osorio Gonzalez, Tiffani Peoples, Michaelle Pollard, Suzan Raechetto-Madrigal, Gabriel Ramos, Cynthia Reyes, Jill Rizlak, Sofia Rombolakis, Linda Romer, Carmen Rowe, Carol Salva, Tonya Schepers, Jennifer A. Schutte, Pushpanjali Sengupta, Michelle Simmonds, Danielle Sirico, Anna Skirvin, Dubraska Stines, Katie Toppel, Nidia Vaz-Correia, Henrietta Vazquez, Rochelle Verstaendig, Jennifer Visalli, Brian Wallrapp, Belinda Walsh, Jill Weatherston, Ashley Whitney, Aaron Wiles, Lisa Wittek, Alexandra Byham Wolf, Sharon Wolkomir, and Quynh Xayarath. I would also like to recognize the many school and district leaders who directly or indirectly supported this project as well, especially Lori Cannetti, Rachel Lindsey, Barbara Noel, Dalimar Rostello, Gregory Scesney, and Rich Taibi.

A special thank-you goes to all my colleagues and friends at Molloy College, who supported this and many other projects, especially Dr. Audrey Cohan, Dr. Maria Dove, and Denise Hughes. Many thanks to Jennifer Delahunt, Denise Hughes, Emily Hughes, Sara Hughes, and Shalinie Sarju for the technical assistance they so patiently offered with the manuscript preparation.

I extend a heartfelt thank-you to my critical friend, Glenda Harrell, who never held back praise nor the much needed critical insights as she read through all the chapters with meticulous attention to detail and who also helped collect exceptional teacher and student work samples in support of this publication.

Last but by all means not least, a huge shout-out to Holly Price Kim, my editor, who invited me to venture into this project, shared my vision for this book from its inception, and guided its creation with unwavering support and true collaboration!

Thank you, readers of this book: I wish you well when working with this population of students. I hope the book offers practical strategies coupled with a rich selection of examples and authentic illustrations that aid you in translating the strategies presented in the book to your own classroom and school.

> A beautiful thing is never perfect.
>
> —EGYPTIAN PROVERB

If you are reading this book, you are likely among the ever-growing group of teachers in the United States who have multilingual students in their classrooms and who face the challenges and joys of guiding them on a journey of cultural, linguistic, and academic explorations. Or you might be a student in a teacher education program, just beginning to explore the complexities of the profession, who eagerly (or perhaps a bit nervously) anticipates what it might be like to work with students who do not speak English (yet!). You might be a coach, school or district administrator, or teacher educator, who is looking for a quick-to-read, user-friendly, accessible resource to address the diverse language and literacy proficiencies that coexist in many classrooms. My wish is that you find what you are looking for in this book.

Some Key Concepts from Language Acquisition

Language acquisition and language learning are strictly separated by some researchers and practitioners. In this book, I suggest that the process of language acquisition and intentional learning in the academic context cannot be artificially separated, thus I tend to refer to them by a common term of *language development*. When I use the term *language proficiency*, I am referring to the child's linguistic competence to process language (such as listen and read) and to produce language (such as speak and write). It is critical to recognize the variations that may occur among students and across language domains. Effective instruction will incorporate students' strengths as well as instructional strategies that support students' knowledge of the language and account for their levels of proficiency. Yet, a word of caution is in order.

Language development is neither static nor linear. Although there are five consecutive chapters depicting language progressions, offering snapshots of students at various stages of their language proficiency, keep in mind that language acquisition is fluid and dynamic. Students come with vast individual differences in their backgrounds and experiences, so at any given moment, some students may exhibit some abilities at a higher proficiency level and other students at a lower one. Language proficiency levels cannot define who a student is; instead, each level simply offers a frame of reference what the student is able to do (Shafer Willner 2013).

To avoid a static notion of student abilities, maintain a flexible and growth-oriented mind-set when working with English learners (ELs) and when reading this book. Use strategies from across multiple chapters to respond to your students' dynamic language development needs (Heritage, Linquanti, and Walqui 2015).

Focusing on what students can do, as opposed to what they cannot do, is more likely to make students feel empowered and able to learn to English. According to a deficit model, students are at an academic disadvantage due to their cultural, social, and linguistic backgrounds, including their lack of or limited ability to communicate in English. In contrast, an assets-based model of education considers and intentionally builds upon the values, lived experiences, language patterns, and background knowledge students bring and sees them as strengths and advantages that support, not hinder, learning. As Walqui and van Lier (2010) sum up, the assets-based approach "looks ahead to what students can become and that builds on the knowledge, beliefs, and values all students bring to school" (x).

Five Basic Premises

This book is built on five tenets that both informed the writing of this book and offer an overarching framework for my work with multilingual learners and their teachers.

1. Assets-Based Philosophy

ELs and their rich cultural and linguistic backgrounds must be recognized as a social and educational resource for everyone in a school community. Rather than looking at ELs as deficient and lacking knowledge and skills, I take a strengths-based approach to understanding what each child is able to do and how to support them all to reach their full potential. An asset-based philosophy of teaching is realized when you build on students' experiences and deeply connect instruction to students' and their families' lives. In this book, what students "can do" will be treated as exactly what the students are supposed to do. We cannot remediate what has not been built yet!

2. Individual Variations

As a group, ELs represent tremendous diversity, not only culturally, linguistically, and socioeconomically but also based on how much prior knowledge and what type of academic, linguistic, and literacy skills they bring with them when they enter your classroom. Although language proficiency tests are commonly administered in each state to establish incoming students' proficiency levels, it is important to understand that students' trajectory and direction of development may be different in the four language domains. In speaking and listening, they may represent one level, and in reading and writing, a quite different one.

Although there are common patterns and predictable stages of language acquisition, ELs are unique individuals who move along the continuum of language learning at different rates. When you work with ELs, you notice that progress students make week to week, or month to month, or year to year will vary. In addition, ELs may appear to have skills associated with more than one language or literacy development stage.

3. Integrated Content, Language, and Literacy Instruction

Language and literacy learning for ELs may not exist in isolation from the academic curriculum (Heritage, Linquanti, and Walqui 2015). Academic language is recognized as the language used in schools to acquire new or deeper understanding of the core curriculum and to communicate that understanding to others (Gottlieb and Ernst-Slavit 2014). With this notion in mind, here I take an approach to introducing strategies that may be used across grade levels and across content areas in support of developing academic language and literacy skills. Pacheco, Daniel, and Pray (2017) suggest that "language and content are not separate, and as students engage with different disciplines, they learn to use language practices valued in that discipline" (75). Language must be seen as a path to and an integral part of whatever content we teach (Hakuta, Santos, and Fang 2013).

4. Culturally and Linguistically Sustaining Instructional and Assessment Practices

In a seminal essay, Django Paris (2012) carefully differentiates between culturally responsive (Ladson-Billing 2011) or culturally proficient philosophies and argues that students need culturally and linguistically sustaining instruction and assessment. Teachers who engage in these practices not only recognize and respond to students' languages, literacies, and cultural practices but also validate them through multimodal and multilingual learning opportunities. The goal is help student become successful in U.S. schools and society but not at the expense of sacrificing their existing cultural and linguistic competences.

5. Purposeful Interaction and Collaboration

Language and literacy development as well as content attainment require students to interact not just with the academic content and their teachers but with each other as well. In the social-constructivist tradition, I recognize that language does not thrive without ample opportunities to participate in meaningful learning activities that require collaboration. Throughout the book, I will emphasize the need for peer interaction, peer-supported learning, and authentic language use, one that organically includes home languages and nonverbal and multimodal representations.

Research-Informed and Evidence-Based Practices

The collection of strategies presented in the five chapters is based on the most current research and evidence-based practices reported by leading researchers and professional organizations. Especially influential are the Practice Guides published by Institute of Education Sciences (Baker et al. 2014) and the research and practitioner-oriented work published by TESOL International Association and WIDA Consortium. I also acknowledge and build upon the vast practitioner knowledge that is represented by the exceptional teacher and student work samples shared in this book.

What You Will Find in This Book

I unpack the five levels of language acquisition one chapter at a time. I emphasize the common characteristics of learners at each stage and present a unique set of strategies to be used with students at each level.

Each chapter starts with two student vignettes that tell the stories of ELs from around the world who settle in the United States and attend kindergarten through grade 8. These composites were inspired by the many stories teachers shared with me over the a past few years.

The next major section of each chapter explores the characteristics of ELs on the target language proficiency level followed by the instructional practices and strategies that support each level. Strategies are organized into five strands—Visual Support, Learning by Doing, Oral Language Production, Reading Support, Writing Support—targeting the five proficiency levels.

Strategies under the Visual Support and Learning by Doing sections will encourage you to consistently supplement language, literacy, and academic content learning via multimodality. Oral Language Production sections will include a rage of peer-supported, small-group learning opportunities that require authentic academic conversations. Saunders and O'Brien (2006) confirmed that "there is no controversy about the fundamental importance of English oral language development as part of the larger enterprise of educating ELLs" (14). Reading and Writing Support will include ways to enhance ELs' literacy development.

To reach the broadest possible audience, the five levels of language proficiency are based on the TESOL framework, since it is similar to both WIDA's and other existing frameworks.

1. *Starting:* being exposed to English with limited language production

2. *Emerging:* demonstrating receptive and emerging productive language skills

3. *Developing:* employing basic oral and written language skills with predictable error patterns

4. *Expanding:* employing more advanced oral and written language skills with fewer errors

5. *Bridging:* approximating native language proficiency.

Although the chapters are organized by language proficiency level, most strategies and recommendations may be adapted and transferred to other proficiency levels as well. Each chapter ends with revisiting the chapter opening vignettes and considering what the students featured in the vignettes would be able to do as they move on to the next proficiency level.

Growing
Language
&
Literacy

Chapter One

Supporting STARTING Level English Learners

Who Are *Starting* Level Students?

Being at the onset of this fascinating journey we formally refer to as *second language acquisition* can be exhilarating and exhausting. Let's meet two students, Cristela and Tamir, who are at the Starting level of second language acquisition. Although they represent different cultural, linguistic, and academic experiences and they attend different schools at different grade levels, they share at least one common characteristic: they are both just beginning to learn English as a new language. As you read their stories, look for cultural, linguistic, and academic assets they possess, and consider how to build upon them. Notice if you have had students with similar backgrounds and responses to schooling in the United States, and reflect on what you would do to help them get started with English. How would you welcome them to your classroom? How would you introduce new concepts and skills in a language yet to be acquired? The goal of this chapter is to offer some insights into first steps of language acquisition.

The beginning is the half of every action.

—GREEK PROVERB

Cristela

Cristela came to the United States from El Salvador when she was five. She attended kindergarten in Texas before moving to Maryland, where she resides with her mother, uncle, and three cousins. Her mother does not read or write in Spanish or English; her uncle, who is more proficient in English, regularly helps with translating.

Cristela was placed in a first-grade cotaught classroom, where she had support from one of her Spanish-speaking classmates and from her newly found English-speaking friends as well. Cristela learned to follow the well-established routines with relative ease, perhaps because her classmates were eager to include her and help her throughout the day. Initially, Cristela nodded and smiled a lot, even when she did not quite understand what was happening around her. At other times she looked confused and approached her teachers or classmates speaking in Spanish. She enjoyed the songs and chants that were shared in the classroom, and after one of those morning meeting chats, she came out of her silent period and began to repeat words and engage in simple conversations.

She received instructional support from the ELD (English language development) teacher three periods each day. There were eight other students in the classroom who spoke Cristela's native language, so Spanish was heard on the playground, during recess, in the lunchroom, and when Cristela worked in groups. Now five months after her arrival, she has begun to learn her letters. She still has difficulty with pronouncing some of the sounds in English, but she works diligently and giggles at times when she cannot quite get a sound right. It is easier for her to enunciate beginning word sounds than ending sounds. Cristela has learned several two- and three-word phrases to accomplish a task; "Can you help me?" is one of them.

Cristela does best when she describes the pictures she has drawn using patterned sentences. She is able to write "I see" sentences and even gets the initial sound of most words correctly using inventive spelling. Although she is still a Starting level student, she has made considerable growth in five short months. She is completing her homework at home with her uncle, who also shared that Cristela is now teaching her mom English!

→ STOP AND REFLECT ←

What were Cristela's greatest assets as a newcomer to the United States? What could her steady progress be attributed to? What would you do to help her further expand her language and literacy skills?

Tamir

Tamir is a twelve-year-old boy from Syria, whose family has suffered greatly since the start of civil war in 2011. He lost his home and several close family members in Aleppo, Syria, when his neighborhood was bombed. Tamir's grandmother and uncle are unaccounted for, but the rest of the family fled to neighboring Jordan. Tamir's father, mother, two siblings, and cousin spent two years in a Zaatari refugee camp, where they lived in a trailer and food and medical supplies were scarce. Although Tamir did well in school and enjoyed reading, art, and studying in general prior to the civil war in Syria, he has not attended school regularly for quite a while. Tamir's father, who was an instructor at the Mamoun University for Science and Technology, tried to help him continue his education, but the lack of appropriate textbooks and school supplies limited the scope of their studying. By pointing to a map, Tamir was able to share that the family migrated through Turkey, Eastern Europe, and Germany on their long journey to the United States. The family was waiting for a visa to allow legal entrance to the United States for a number of years and went through several rounds of screening before finally they were admitted six months ago. Now in the United States, Tamir attends seventh grade in a newcomer center, which is specially designed to welcome kindergarten to eighth-grade students and support them with the vast cultural and linguistic shifts they experience when they first arrive in the United States.

He understands basic commands and directions, especially when his teacher uses gestures and visual cues. Two months after his arrival, he has not yet spoken in English to any of his peers or teachers, but he pays more attention in class and does not always sit alone in the cafeteria any more. He has a buddy who taught him how to use the locker, and he quickly learned the routines of the day. He most enjoys art projects and his science classes, where he can watch his teachers show him what to do.

→ STOP AND REFLECT ←
Why is it important to understand the complex experiences that Tamir brings to school? In what ways should Tamir's teachers respond to the trauma that he has lived through? What assets can his teachers tap into? What would you do to help him thrive in middle school after he leaves the newcomer center?

What's in a Name?

As the label suggests, Starting level students are in a unique position. When they enter the U.S. school system and are assessed for language proficiency, they may produce minimal, formulaic language ("thank you," "hello") in English or nothing at all, and they may not recognize what is being spoken or read to them. They may be able to identify some written words that are internationally known (for example, the stop sign, some logos such as Coca-Cola, names of common tech tools like iPad, and so on). These children have vast life and literacy experiences connected to another language and culture, so welcoming them as resources and assets in the school and classroom community is important.

Since many—though not all—of them are recent arrivals, they are likely to benefit from predictable routines and structures. With careful scaffolding, ample visual support, and background knowledge (that they either possess or you build about everyday topics or academic content), they can gain an overall understanding of what is presented in class. They begin to use words, phrases, and short sentences that they may have memorized as a chunk of language (e.g., "May I go to the bathroom?") with increasing confidence. They are just starting to develop foundational language and literacy skills in English, hence the name *Starting*.

Some students may start out on the same level for the four key language domains, namely listening, speaking, reading, and writing; others may have some receptive skills, gained through familiarity with popular songs, movies, or video games. Yet others might have lived all their lives in the United States but had limited exposure to formal English. Soon enough, you can observe that they are beginning to understand and process what is happening around them, what is being spoken or read to them. Make sure you observe all four language skills and notice how their receptive skills (especially listening) tend to develop more rapidly than the productive language skills (speaking and writing). The trajectory of certain literacy skills is also predictable: basic decoding may come earlier than developing reading comprehension skills, yet visuals help understand any lesson. See Figure 1.1 for an example of how Cydnie Jorgenson uses a Flow Map to review what to do when you go on a bear hunt. Previously, her first graders brainstormed what they would need to take on a hike, then they watched a video and sequenced steps of going on a bear hunt. Notice the Circle Map of "Things You Need to Go on a Hike" that she created in collaboration with her students. (See more on Thinking Maps in Chapter 4.)

Most of your students will demonstrate accelerated growth and rapid advancement to the next level called Emerging (see Chapter 2), whereas some will need additional time to reveal the progress they are making. Keep the following "mantra" in mind: *"lower is faster, higher is slower"* (Cook et al. 2008, 7). This research-informed principle suggests that English learners (ELs) in lower grades (younger students) and those who are at lower proficiency levels (Starting and Emerging, and even Developing) acquire language at faster rates, whereas upper elementary and middle school

Figure 1.1   Visually Enriched Classroom Environment

students or those at the Developing and Expanding levels or above will experience a slower rate of growth. Patience and perseverance—yours and theirs—are much-needed resources!

As you can see in Figure 1.2, the *Starting* level of language proficiency has many other labels depending on the theoretical framework you refer to, the state or country you live in, or the language development standards you use. Keep in mind that the descriptions for each category by the various professional organizations might not completely overlap.

Starting Level by Other Labels		
TESOL	**Hill and Miller (2014)**	**WIDA**
Starting	Preproduction	Entering

ELPA (2016)	**New York**	**California**	**Texas**
Emerging	Entering	Emerging	Beginner

Figure 1.2

What Can We Learn from Research?

The stage of language acquisition referred to as *Starting* in this book was first described as preproduction by Krashen and Terrell (1983). The preproduction stage (sometimes referred to as the silent period) may last up to six months, and it is often characterized by—as its name suggests—accumulating receptive language skills but not yet producing any or much in spoken or written form. Not all Starting level students may need several months to advance to the next level, so individual variances are to be expected. In fact, Gibbons (2006) considers this preverbal stage a challenging period that should not last longer than a month; through patterns and routines, most children will emerge from it relatively quickly. Similarly, Ohta (2001) reminds us that the "seemingly silent learner is neither passive nor disengaged, but is involved in an intrapersonal interactive process" (12). Most recently, Bligh (2014) has studied the silent period of young bilingual learners from a sociocultural perspective. Her study concludes with emphasizing the important role educators play in mediating and providing alternative modes of learning while embracing the learners' private speech (internal thoughts and silent participation in learning). Figure 1.3 shows how Leah Leonard engages her fourth- and fifth-grade Starting level students (who are also designated as SIFE, or students with interrupted formal education) to help them think about the different kinds of jobs that protect people.

Research has also well documented that Starting level students' native languages are critical resources. An important finding from research on bilingualism is especially relevant for ELs who do not yet communicate in English. Cummins (2001) firmly believes that "to reject a child's language in the school is to reject the child" (19). Similarly, Christensen (2010) suggests that "by bringing students' languages from their homes into the classroom, we validate their culture and their history as topics worthy of study" (33). A key research-informed practice is to

Figure 1.3 Visual Anchor Chart About Jobs

create a supportive environment for all students by valuing not just bilingualism in the individual but plurilingualism in the community and by making all students' languages visible and valued (Agirdag 2009). When students' home languages are used and affirmed in school, their emergent bilingual and bicultural identities are also affirmed, and the bridge to learning English is established. Finally, Goldenberg (2013) summarized key strategies that teachers may use to support English acquisition through home language strategies.

→ Use cognates or words that look and sound similar as well as have the same or very similar meaning.

→ Offer a brief explanation in the home language prior to instruction in English.

→ Use the home language for previewing and reviewing the lesson (while the lesson is taught in English).

→ Teach literacy or cognitive strategies in the home language, and provide opportunities to transfer those strategies when using English.

Many teachers pay close attention to building a multilingual environment in their classrooms. See Figure 1.4 for a selection of labels Elena Dokshansky co-created with her multilingual colleagues and her fourth-grade students to validate and support their multiple home languages and to help them learn key concepts.

Figure 1.4 Multilingual Labels

What Can *Starting* Level English Learners Do?

Although most *Starting* level students are newcomers to the United States, some, especially in kindergarten, may have grow up in rich cultural and linguistic contexts their parents provided in the home languages, and they might have had exposure to U.S. cultural and linguistic experiences. It is important to know whether your student is a U.S.-born child, someone who has only known the United States as his or her home, or whether the family had to uproot and leave behind everything the child knew and felt comfortable with. When you welcome ELs, put yourself in their shoes and consider—through the eyes of each child—what their first impressions are. If they don't understand your verbal input, they will certainly be more responsive to nonverbal cues: your body language, facial impressions, smile, gestures, tone of voice, and so on.

Let's flip the coin: What are your first impressions? What do you first notice about ELs at the Starting level? Tung (2013) cautions us not to view "ELL [English language learner] education as a problem, dilemma, achievement gap, or crisis"; instead, she urges us to "embrace ELLs as the very community members who, when well educated, will be the bicultural, bilingual leaders who improve our city neighborhoods and help us participate effectively in the global economy" (4). With this asset-based—rather than deficiency-oriented—philosophy, let's look at what positive expectations you can have for Starting level students, or as aptly put by WIDA (2012), what these students *can do*. These accomplishments are not expected on the very first day; they develop over the course of many days and weeks or even months.

When it comes to *listening*, you can expect students to begin to show evidence of comprehending English by doing the following:

> → respond with gestures rather than words (nodding, shaking their heads, making hand gestures)
>
> → respond nonverbally to simple, frequently used classroom commands ("Come here!")
>
> → point to familiar objects around the classroom
>
> → identify classmates by their names
>
> → become familiar with the sounds and rhythms of the English language

- → recognize everyday classroom language (words and short phrases) associated with daily routines (*homework, open your books, line up, do now*)
- → point to words or phrases that have been previously introduced and are part of the environmental print in the classroom and school (*exit sign, homework*)
- → recognize and respond to formulaic language ("Hello"; "Thank you"; "How are you?").

Regarding *speaking* skills, you will notice that students initially respond and communicate nonverbally by nodding or gesturing, pointing to objects or visuals, or attempting to communicate in their native language. They will incrementally expand their English-speaking skills by doing the following:

- → offer one-word answers such as "yes" or "no"
- → translanguage or code-switch (using their native language with some English words) for communication in response to English prompts (see more discussion of translanguaging in Chapter 2)
- → repeat words and phrases commonly used in familiar settings
- → name objects found around the classroom and school by names
- → call their teachers and classmates by name
- → use formulaic language ("I don't understand"; "Help me, please")
- → participate in short songs and chants that they are able to memorize (especially if there are hand gestures or motions).

When it comes to *reading*, students are likely to be nonreaders in English, yet they are anticipated to develop some foundational skills such as the following:

- → read environmental print (exit sign, classroom labels, anchor chart headings)
- → rely on visual support for understanding what is read aloud to them
- → recognize letters
- → make letter-sound connections

→ recognize high-frequency words

→ enjoy read-alouds that are well supported with visuals, hand motions, and other nonverbal supports

→ use bilingual dictionaries to look up words.

Finally, in the area of *writing,* students may begin to do the following:

→ form letters

→ print frequently used words including their names and headings

→ copy words

→ draw pictures

→ create illustrations or other graphic representations of their ideas with word labels in English

→ write in their native language (if literate), and add labels or key words in English.

Figure 1.5 Penguin Made out of Construction Paper

Amy Eckelmann's and Jessica Houston's Starting level kindergarten student loves to express his new learning through drawing, writing, and using artistic expressions. See Figure 1.5 and Figure 1.6 for his responses to the lesson about penguins. Notice how successfully he uses the various scaffolds available to him when he formulates one of his first sentences ever produced in writing.

Consider your expectations for *Starting* level students. They need meaningful exposure to English to begin to comprehend and respond to what is presented in your classroom. They are most likely to succeed and progress when support is given in *multiple* ways, *multiple* languages, and *multiple* modalities. For example, I would engage Cristela from the beginning of the chapter in all the languages available to her. She will build English language skills through guided reading lessons and purposeful classroom discussions that include Spanish and English language use. She can use simple sentences to explain what she has read with the help of sentence starters and patterned language. To support Tamir, I would create a range of meaningful hands-on learning opportunities as well as ways for him to express his ideas artistically. Although he may not be able to use English at the seventh-grade level, I would need to give him every chance to think at grade level as he encounters complex content through visuals, digital media, and multilingual resources.

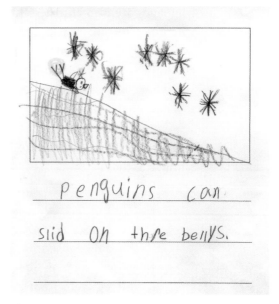

Figure 1.6 Illustration and Writing About Penguins

What Practices Support *Starting* Level Students?

Starting level students will be best supported through teaching techniques that are multidimensional linguistically and academically. They need learning activities that allow them to be fully engaged by listening to others (both teachers and peers) talk about something they can relate to. When it comes to contributing to class, find ways for students to do so with minimal language use such as expressing themselves nonverbally, visually, artistically, through movement, and so on. If literate in the native language, encouraging students to use that language as a bridge to English is critical for cultural, social-emotional, and linguistic development.

When you have a student at the Starting level in your class, make sure that he or she feels welcome and included in the classroom and school community. Three practices to implement are (1) using what is familiar to your new students as a primary source of or link to learning, (2) establishing a peer support system, and (3) building basic comprehension and communicative language in English.

Capitalize on Familiarity

Starting level students more than any other group of ELs must be made to feel that they belong and can learn English while their home cultures and native languages are also affirmed. Imagine that you are seven and move to a place where not too many people know the games and sports you have grown up with, books that your mother read aloud to you as bedtime stories, the customs and holidays that your family cherish, the songs or soft whispers that comforted you when you got hurt, or the food that nourished you. How would you adjust to a new environment?

One powerful way you can welcome newcomers is by making them feel a sense of belonging and incorporating resources into your teaching that will be familiar to them.

→ Learn to say the child's name correctly.

→ Learn some phrases such as "Welcome," "Glad to see you," "I am your teacher" in the child's home language. (Several apps, such as Google Translate, iTranslate, Papago, SayHi, Speak and Translate, Textgrabber, Waygo, are helpful to translate expressions and short sentences with increasing accuracy from English to just about any language.)

→ Create a word wall that has some key concepts in every language represented in your classroom. Some powerful words might include *friendship*, *respect*, *learning*. See Figure 1.7 for a multilingual word wall (inspired by Naomi Barbour's similar color-coded word walls for high school ELs) with key vocabulary from the novel *Esmeralda Rising* (in Polish, Spanish, Chinese, and Russian).

→ During recess, play music or provide games and activities that represent students' home lives and experiences.

→ Use images that your Starting level students can recognize.

→ When establishing classroom routines and procedures, incorporate print and visual cues.

→ Teach words and phrases directly related to the class and school environment. Thorpe (2017) also suggests to "use the students' immediate surroundings to expand their vocabulary" (18). See Figures 1.8 and 1.9 for how Nidia Vaz-Correia's sixth-grade students learn about prepositions as the classroom comes alive with labels.

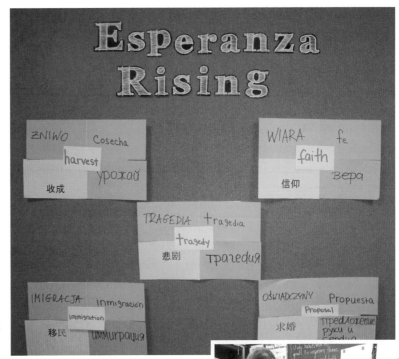

Figure 1.7
Color-Coded
Multilingual
Word Wall

Figure 1.8   Prepositions in the Classroom

Figure 1.9   Prepositions in the Classroom

Moll (1992) has long recognized that all students come to school with tremendous knowledge derived from home- and community-based shared experiences that are often unrelated to the taught curriculum and skills needed for academic success. Moll calls this *funds of knowledge*. When the knowledge students accumulate at home or through their vast out-of-school experiences is connected to who they are, the term used is *funds of identity*. Esteban-Guitart and Moll (2014) suggest that "funds of knowledge—bodies of knowledge and skills that are essential for the well-being of an entire household—become funds of identity when people actively use them to define themselves" (31). When we recognize students' funds of knowledge, we encourage them to feel valued by connecting their learning with the cultural knowledge they bring to school. Funds of knowledge and funds of identity are rich "tool kits" (73) created from the students' lived experiences.

When a newcomer enters your classrooms, embrace what they know and who they are, and consider them as a major source of information. Use their experiences as a way to bridge to the curriculum, the new culture, and the language they are about to acquire (Helman, Rogers, Frederick, and Struck 2016). Consider all the ways you can help your ELs see aspects of their out-of-school cultural and linguistic experiences reflected in the school environment and the learning activities. Some of these suggestions impact the larger school community, so your role might be to advocate on behalf of ELs to ensure the following:

→ Have signs around the building welcoming students and families in all the languages spoken in the community.

→ Prepare information booklets or family handbooks available in all the languages spoken in the community.

→ Make sure school staff feel comfortable greeting and interacting with adults who do not speak English well, using cues and resources that illustrate frequently communicated processes.

→ Be sure that ELs see their own and their classmates' work written in multiple languages on bulletin boards.

→ Make books and digital media available in languages other than English.

→ Make interpreters available on site or on call as needed to support family meetings.

→ Have student ambassadors who welcome new students into the school community, offer tours of the building, and join the new student at recess and other unstructured times (Fisher and Frey 2017).

→ Let students tell their personal stories, make connections to text—both fiction and nonfiction—and make sense of their way of life at home.

Replicate or expand some of these school-wide practices, and welcome your beginners with multilingual signs and resources in your classroom. English-speaking students may create welcome cards or special placemats that include key sentences or phrases and visuals students can point to. See Figure 1.10 for a three-dimensional map that a fifth grader created to help his classmates better understand the "lay of the land."

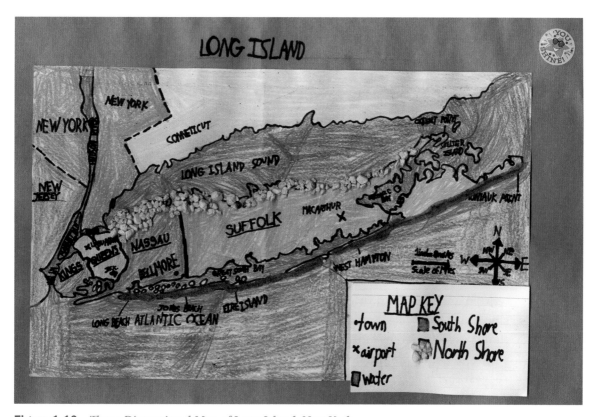

Figure 1.10 Three-Dimensional Map of Long Island, New York

A newcomer kit or welcome kit may be a helpful source with some key information (Colorín Colorado n.d.; Law and Eckes 2010).

→ how to navigate the school: a colorful map that shows where to find some key places (bathrooms, nurse's room, cafeteria)

→ how to find the child's classroom: classroom location and teacher's name and phone number or email

→ routines regarding arrival and dismissal—especially if bussing is involved and ELs need to find their way to the correct school bus

→ routines and expectations about snack and lunchtime

→ a list of key community-based organizations and resources such as names and numbers of other families who have volunteered to offer help

→ a basic English dictionary of key words, phrases, and sentences translated into the child's home language.

See a newcomer kit table of contents by Michelle D'Errico in Figure 1.11 and a section from Gabriel Ramos' newcomer kit in Figure 1.12. Also see visual guidance to the school section in Sofia Rombolakis' newcomer toolkit in Figure 1.13.

Establish a Peer Support System

When you have a new student in your classroom, regardless of the age or background, that child is likely to face some challenges as he or she begins to adjust to the new school and classroom environment, accept the changes in routines, understand the social and academic expectations, adhere to the written and unwritten rules of, make new friends, and build trust in relationships with both peers and adults. When your new student is an EL, the situation is exacerbated by cultural and linguistic differences, so an important first step is to help the child develop a sense of belonging. Fisher and Frey (2017) suggest that you seat new students so they "maximize the connections [they] can make with peers" (83). Building relationships one classmate at a time can

For the Parents/Para los Padres

For the Student/Para el Estudiante

Figure 1.11 Newcomer Kit Table of Contents

VOCABULARY | VOCABULARIO

CLASSROOM EXPRESSIONS - TEACHER | EXPRESIONES DE LA CLASE - PROFESOR

Sit down	Siéntense or Siéntate
Raise your hand	Levanten or Levanta la mano
Take out (your homework, iPad, etc)	Saquen or Saca (la tarea, su iPad, etc)
A volunteer to…	Un voluntario para…
Try	Try
Ready?	¿Listos?
Close (the door, the window, etc)	Cierren or Cierra (la puerta, la ventana)
Open (the door, the window, etc)	Abran or Abre (la puerta, la ventana)

CLASSROOM EXPRESSIONS - STUDENT | EXPRESIONES DE LA CLASE - ALUMNO

How do you say…..?	¿Cómo se dice…?
How do you spell…?	¿Cómo se escribe…?
What does … mean?	¿Qué quiere decir…?
Slower, please.	Más lento, por favor.
Can you explain, please?	¿Puedes explicar en inglés, por favor?
Can I go to the bathroom?	¿Puedo ir al baño?
Can I get a drink of water?	¿Puedo beber agua?
I don't know.	No sé.

Figure 1.12 A Bilingual Page from a Newcomer Kit

Welcome to 4ᵗʰ Grade!
Ms. Rombolakis

I am your fourth grade teacher, Ms. Rombolakis. This year you will learn about various different topics, as well as develop your reading and math skills! Over the course of this school year we will learn about Native American tribes, their culture, and their natural resources. We will learn to create museum exhibits and become incredible researchers! We will also become very strong mathematicians. We will be learning about angles, double digit multiplication, long division, and so much more! I look forward to having you in my class this year, and I am excited for us to all work together and learn as much as we can.

Soy su maestra de cuarto grado, la Sra. Rombolakis. Este año aprenderás sobre varios temas diferentes, ¡y también desarrollarás tus habilidades de lectura y matemáticas! En el transcurso de este año escolar, aprenderemos sobre las tribus nativas, su cultura y sus recursos naturales. ¡Aprenderemos a crear exhibiciones de museos y nos convertiremos en increíbles investigadores! También nos convertiremos en matemáticos muy fuertes. Aprenderemos sobre ángulos, multiplicación de dos dígitos, división larga y mucho más. Espero tenerte en mi clase este año, y estoy entusiasmado de que trabajemos juntos y aprendamos todo lo que podamos.

Important Notes | Puntos Importantes:
E-mail: srombolakis@ps171.org **Correo Electrónico:** srombolakis@ps171.org
Phone Number: (212) 860-5801 **Número de Teléfono:** (212) 860-5801
Extra Help: Wednesday & Thursday: 2:20PM-3:00PM **Ayuda Extra:** Miércoles y Jueves: 2:20PM-3:00PM

Figure 1.13 Helping Newcomers Learn About Their New Teacher and New School

Welcome ! | ¡Bienvenido!

Welcome to P.S.171! We are very excited to welcome you into our school community. Below you will find our school website. On our website you have access to the contact information of the school staff, class websites, helpful resources for students to access, and important information for parents. Feel free to familiarize yourself with the website.

Bienvenido a P.S.171! Estamos muy emocionados de darle la bienvenida a nuestra comunidad escolar. A continuación encontrará nuestro sitio web de la escuela. En nuestro sitio web tiene acceso a la información de contacto del personal de la escuela, los sitios web de las clases, los recursos útiles para el acceso de los alumnos y la información importante para los padres. Siéntase libre de familiarizarse con el sitio web.

School Website | Sitio Web
www.ps171.org
(212) 860 – 5801
19 103rd St, New York, NY 10029

be achieved in a more systematic way if you assign various roles to a number of peers in the classroom.

A **classroom helper** will do just what its name suggests: be attentive to the needs of the student regarding classroom routines and instructional activities such as when it is time to line up, transition to a new class, get ready for lunch, and so on.

A **literacy partner** will whisper-read to the EL during silent reading time and share his or her writing with the EL while also offering encouragement for native language use.

A **math** (or **social studies** or **science**) **associate** will sit with the newcomer during math (or social studies or science) class to help navigate the resources.

A **homework tracker** will ensure that the appropriate (differentiated) homework goes home with the EL.

Figure 1.14 Reading buddies support each other sorting picture cards about loud and soft sounds.

It is helpful if the buddy system includes children that speak the same language as your newcomer, but it may not be possible in many classrooms. It is always a good idea to ask students to volunteer to be a buddy and to select ones who are known to be patient, empathetic, and more than willing to take risks and learn from their peers. Also, remember to regularly check in with the partners and change them up so more students to have the opportunity to help. Based on the class dynamics, you may want to create a buddy system that includes all students and/or rotate the partners to expand the opportunities for positive student-to-student interactions. Partnering ELs with others is a strong way to build peer acceptance and leadership skills among the more proficient students in the class and enhance a positive class culture where everyone is able to thrive. Figure 1.14 shows a pair of reading buddies in Michelle Castor and Caroline Brokaw's cotaught first-grade classroom and Figure 1.15

Claudia Leon's seventh-grade students collaborating on making illustrated social studies word books.

Build Basic Comprehension and Communication Skills

At the very onset of language acquisition, your Starting level ELs will want to understand what is happening around them and learn how to communicate their needs. How can you help them develop language skills to respond to their immediate needs?

Figure 1.15 Students work together to create instructional materials for themselves.

→ Attach language to objects and actions. For students in younger grades, when you pick up a book, say, "Book" or "This is your book" and repeat the command "Pick up your book," allowing the beginner ELs to hear the words that are connected to objects and actions commonly used in the classroom. For students in upper grades, prepare illustrated anchor charts that include key vocabulary.

→ Create a daily schedule (elementary) or an agenda (middle school) that is visually supported with diagrams or pictures. Not only will your ELs develop familiarity with the structure of the day and understand what is expected of them, but they will also learn—first to recognize and then to articulate— some key words and phrases. See Figure 1.16 for a morning routine checklist designed for a first-grade class.

Figure 1.16 First-Grade Morning Checklist with Visuals

What Strategies Will Help *Starting* Level Students Most?

The strategies that are woven throughout the book will offer some foundational skills for Starting level students. An important word of caution: many of these strategies may be used on all levels of language proficiency so as you read through the book try to avoid limiting your strategy use to the designated language proficiency levels where they were first introduced.

Visual Support

Visual support for beginner language learners is a lifesaver. No visual is powerful enough to replace the real objects, however; so whenever possible, use realia (actual artifacts that students can see, touch, feel, smell, and examine in close proximity) or manipulatives that are either commercially made or produced by teachers and students. Students in Michaelle Pollard's fourth-grade classroom supported by Caroline Brokaw were learning about conduits. For ELs who didn't have the English vocabulary for all the objects, Caroline created a resource by putting the actual objects on a sheet of paper and adding labels (see Figure 1.17). She also made photocopies for students to keep with them as they worked with their partner during the investigation.

It has been well established that creating a language-rich, vibrant environment significantly contributes to language and literacy development for all students (Gottlieb and Ernst-Slavin 2014; Zwiers 2014). For Starting ELs, making language visible is a must, especially when realia are not available for every topic you teach. Look around your classroom and assess ways you can create or enrich the learning environment visually by creating illustrated word walls,

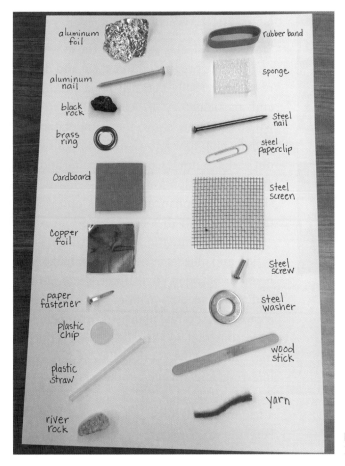

Figure 1.17 A Science Realia Reference Sheet

posting sentence frames for oral and written communication, or enhancing charts. In Figure 1.18 you can see Katie Toppel's interactive labeled diagram with word cards she uses with first graders. Figure 1.19 shows Hilary Moss' illustrated character traits chart prepared with her fourth-grade students.

You can further enhance comprehension through rebuses in which key words have illustrations above them. Although originally intended for students with special needs, the Boardmaker software or the Web-based version at www.boardmakeronline.com allows you to design schedules, instructional materials, and other even multilingual tools with consistent symbols for easier communication. In another class learning about plants, Ashley Whitney created rebuses for *Starting* level students so they, too, could understand how plants grow (Figure 1.20).

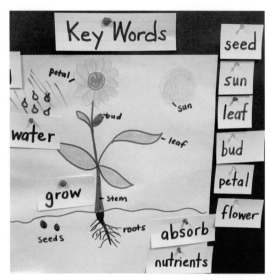

Figure 1.18 Labeled Diagram Combined with Interactive Word Cards

Figure 1.19 Illustrated Anchor Chart to Distinguish Physical and Personality Traits

Learning by Doing

Starting level ELs, especially those who remain in the preproduction stage and do not respond verbally yet, are most productive and participatory in classroom activities when they can show their understanding and develop new knowledge and skills without verbal output. Content learning and language acquisition for newcomer ELs will be significantly enhanced if hands-on explorations are included.

When we intentionally attach language to action and objects, it helps ELs to make connections between English words and phrases and the concepts, qualities, or actions they represent. Add real objects or manipulatives to lessons that require describing, sequencing, measuring, comparing, contrasting, inferring, and a range of other skills that students must develop. For example, if you teach a lesson on mixtures and solutions, verbally label the various substances and add gestures to indicate what *mixing, settling,* and *dissolving* mean.

Within the early childhood context, use puppets, games, costumes, and toys to create a learning environment that invites authentic usage both for the items you use in the classroom and the language that goes with those gamelike activities. With students in the upper grades, use age-appropriate games that invite them to use their critical thinking and are respectful of their cognitive levels and interests. In Figure 1.21, Ashley Whitney's kindergarteners use shaving cream to try spelling some words. In Figure 1.22,

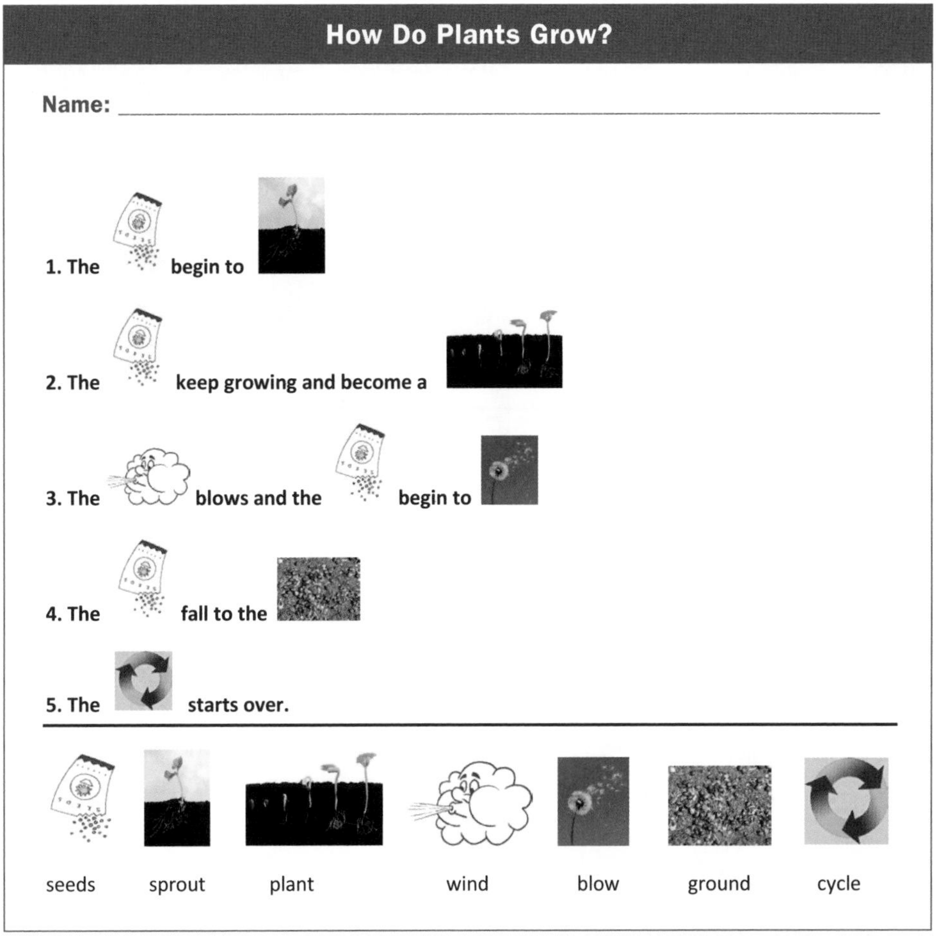

How Do Plants Grow?

Name: _____

1. The [seeds] begin to [sprout]

2. The [seeds] keep growing and become a [plant]

3. The [wind] blows and the [seeds] begin to [blow]

4. The [seeds] fall to the [ground]

5. The [cycle] starts over.

| seeds | sprout | plant | wind | blow | ground | cycle |

Figure 1.20 Rebus Story About Plants

Caroline Brokaw's and Michelle Castor's students work together to explore a variety of materials to determine and record which materials will allow light to pass through and which ones will not. Claudia Leon's middle school students use Legos for practicing descriptive language in Figure 1.23.

When the anxiety about being in a new environment and learning a new language is reduced, Starting level ELs may become much more receptive to English. Games and gamelike learning lower the affective filter first discussed by Krashen (1982) and invite ELs to be more receptive to new experiences with the language.

Figure 1.21 Shaving Cream Spelling in Kindergarten

Figure 1.22 Science Explorations in First Grade

Figure 1.23 Legos support language building.

Total Physical Response, as suggested by the name of this strategy, requires students to respond nonverbally to what is being asked or modeled, such as using a motion or gestures, mimicking what the teacher or the leader of the activity does, or responding to a command with gestures and actions. Variations of the strategy have been used for decades (see first mention by Asher [1981]) to introduce vocabulary, to participate in storytelling through movement, and to enhance beginner language learners' active engagement. If you want to adapt it for your classroom, you have a lot of choices and opportunities for creative implementation.

1. Make it look and sound like the game Simon Says, without tricking the ELs; instead, simply ask them to perform certain actions.

2. Create foldables or other student-made manipulatives that will turn into learning tools.

3. Have them act out parts of a story, be it fiction or nonfiction.

4. Have all students respond nonverbally using thumbs up/ thumbs down for agreeing and disagreeing with a statement, or raising one hand for *yes* and two hands for *no*, and so on.

Oral Language Development

Some Starting level ELs begin to communicate and participate in the classroom in a relatively short period of time—within weeks, days, or even hours after first being introduced to English. Whenever available, establish bilingual peer bridges (pairing up the Starting level EL with a peer who speaks the same native language but is more proficient in English) to ensure your student has someone to talk to both in the shared language and in English. An important caveat to keep in mind is that the peer is not used for translation/interpretation services. Simultaneous translation of instruction by a peer is not a viable scaffold; so have a range of strategies ready!

The initial verbal expressions to expect from Starting level ELs in English are frequently repeated from what they hear you and their classmates say ("Good morning!" "Yes, please!" "No, thank you!" "See you later!") or what they are prompted to say when modeling, gesturing, ample repetition, and support are offered ("My name is _____." "I come from _____." "I am _____ years old."). Next, they are likely to learn formulaic English that goes beyond simple greetings and polite phrases. Aguilar (2016) suggests creating opportunities for ELs to repeat certain sentence structures, such as "I feel _____ today," as they look at a poster or photo-cards depicting a range of emotions and learn to express their feelings. Structured, scaffolded opportunities to add single words to sentence frames will build oral language in ELs.

Yet, ELs will begin to speak when there are authentic opportunities to share ideas. What are some ways to add authenticity to the classroom? Try these ideas:

→ Find out what your Starting level EL is mostly interested in: Is it a sport or hobby? Does he or she have a special skill or talent? What does he or she spend free time doing? Incorporate elements of those special interests into lessons or tasks to make sure your student sees himself or herself in the curriculum presented by you.

→ Use learning centers or stations where students work in small groups to solve a common problem or contribute to meeting a shared goal. For example, see Figure 1.24 for Nidia Vaz-Correia's sixth graders engaged in the marshmallow challenge. Even if Starting level ELs will be at the receptive end of the peer conversation at the onset, eventually they will begin to contribute ideas in a smaller, safer environment.

→ In addition to academic learning centers, create interest-based learning opportunities that include your Starting level ELs' special interests, skills, and knowledge.

→ Invite your Starting level ELs to share something about their lives, families, cultural background, or countries of birth with the class in their native language (with appropriate translation and interpretation using a peer or parent volunteer). This will demonstrate to the class the cultural capital and expertise the child has, thus increasing his or her status among peers and opening up opportunities for questions and interactions.

Figure 1.24 Students succeed when they work together.

→ Use technological tools (iPad, iPhone videos) to capture the child's first words and celebrate the progress through weekly recordings (with student and parent permission). In Figure 1.25, see Michelle Gill's kindergarten student use a tablet to record and share her ideas before she is ready to write them.

Figure 1.25 A kindergarten student records her ideas.

Reading Support

It is important to distinguish learning the mechanics of reading (letter-sound correspondence, word recognition, managing text structure, and so on) from the language and cognitive demands of reading and developing comprehension (Massaro 2017). ELs, just as all learners, need to develop foundational reading skills, which include the ability to:

→ demonstrate understanding of basic features of print and the organization of text

→ know and apply phonics and word-analysis skills to decode words

→ understand spoken words and syllables, and make connections between sounds (phonemes) and letters representing them

→ read with sufficient accuracy and fluency to support comprehension.

Beginning to teach these skills explicitly and systematically to Starting level ELs at the literacy level where they are is a must. Depending on the level of literacy in their native language and the age and grade level of the students, Starting level ELs' progression with reading skills may vary significantly. ELs who have advanced literacy skills in their native language may be able to transfer many of the foundational skills, thus their reading development may be accelerated.

Teaching reading to ELs should never be done in an isolated, fragmented fashion. Instead, "instruction in Foundation Skills should occur in concert with instruction related to Reading, Writing, Speaking and Listening, and Language" (IRA CCSS Committee 2012, 2). Foundational skills are certainly critical to reading comprehension for a variety of reasons (Cunningham and Allington 2011). One of their strongest arguments is the attention factor: "Our brains can attend to a limited number of things at a time. If most of our attention is focused on decoding the words, there is little attention left for the comprehension part of reading" (49). Yet, meaning making and enjoyment must be a key focus in every literacy lesson for ELs to nurture motivation and interest in developing reading skills. How to achieve this? Here are some strategies you might try:

→ Use a range of prereading strategies that are rich in visuals (pictures, videos, realia, visual concept maps, photographs) to set the stage for understanding the gist of the reading.

→ Preview the text using picture walks or text tours.

→ Introduce rhymes, songs, and chants that are easy to memorize (anchor charts or printouts should provide the words for following along).

→ Read aloud to a small group of students with frequent pauses for comprehension checks.

→ Use ample visual support while you are read aloud.

→ Use parallel texts that ELs can read in their native language or listen to as audio recordings.

→ With younger grades, when reading predictable text with recurring segments, try choral responses or choral reading.

→ Use digital texts that offer the option of reading aloud to students while they follow along as well as offer multilingual translations.

Figure 1.26 A third grader listens to a story being read aloud on an iPad.

See Figure 1.26 for example of how, in Bethel Aster's third-grade classroom, ELs have access to digital stories in English and in the native languages of the students.

Writing Support

Fluency in English is not a prerequisite to writing. In fact, you cannot wait until ELs develop full language proficiency to begin to write. Copying—although helpful for practicing letter formation—is not meaningful unless the students fully understand what they are copying and have a chance to add their own ideas to the notes. From the day of their arrival, ELs need explicit instruction in writing that combines the mechanics of writing with writing with an authentic purpose, using both the product and process approaches to instruction. Encourage your Starting level ELs to express themselves in writing using their native languages or respond in developmentally appropriate ways using multiple modalities and languages and media. Cummins (2017) suggests integrating writing and sketching for all students when nonfiction topics are explored. Starting ELs will especially benefit when they can respond to tasks by drawing,

Figure 1.27   Student-Rendered Setting of a Korean Folktale

combining speaking and drawing using technological tools, integrating drawing and writing, listing words and phrases, adding annotations in the language of their choice to drawings they prepared or illustrations you offered, and creating graphic representations of what they have learned or understood in their native language and English. See Figure 1.27 for a sixth-grade student's work in response to Rochelle Verstaendig's lesson on identifying settings and illustrating multicultural folk tales.

For all writing tasks, offer finished models for students to see what the expectations are. Whenever possible, also show the process of how to produce the writing you are expecting by modeling the steps. Create an anchor chart or establish peer support to help guide Starting level ELs. In addition, model how graphic organizers may be used to record key details in the lesson. See Figure 1.28 for a list of appropriate writing activities and Figures 1.29 and 1.30 for work samples from Starting level students in Hilary Moss' and Alex Wolf's classes, respectively.

Writing Opportunities for ELs at the Starting Level

Kind of Writing	Description/Purpose	Tip
All About Me books	Students can share about their lives, their families, their passions, and their interests.	Offer finished models so students can see what they are working toward as well as templates to follow that clearly indicate what each page may focus on.
Artistic expressions	Students can respond to a task or prompt by creating a visual or artistic response.	Invite students to add words, such as labels, captions, or thought bubbles, to combine drawings or other forms of visual arts with words.
Patterned writing	Students can produce a lot of writing even at the Starting level if the basic sentence frame is familiar to them and they can reapply the frame to multiple sentences.	Read books with patterned language or introduce a sentence frame and use a word wall to scaffold student writing.
Photo projects	Students can create photo collages, montages, or photo essays with or without English or native language text.	Provide picture cutouts from magazines or print images. If students bring photos from home, offer to make copies so they can keep the original.
Bilingual dialogue journal	Students use both their native language, drawings, and English to communicate with each other or their teachers through a notebook or journal.	If you are bilingual or multilingual, this is a very powerful way to communicate with your students. Respond to the students bilingually, adding a few words in English to sufficiently challenge them.
Personal dictionary	Students look for key words and phrases and create a bilingual glossary with illustrations.	Give ELs a special notebook where they can collect—and develop ownership of—words and phrases they have learned and want to remember.

Figure 1.28

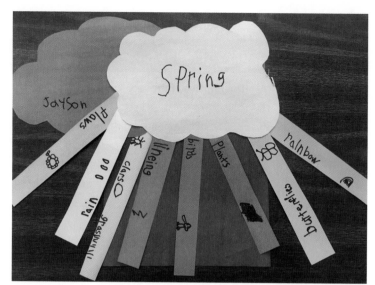

Figure 1.29
Kindergartener's
Visual-Verbal
Response About
What Spring Is

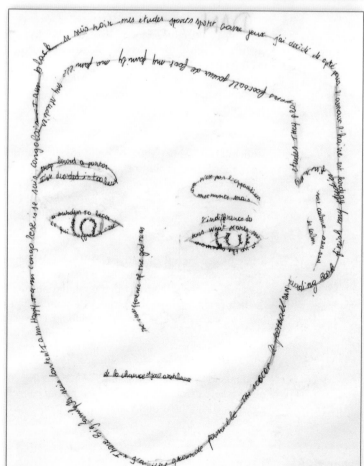

Figure 1.30
Eighth Grader's
Self-Portrait
Freewrite (Home
Language
Encouraged)

When Are *Starting* Level Students Ready to Move On?

Although most schools determine levels of language proficiency and student placement based on annual standardized assessments such as ACCESS by WIDA, ELPA21, and NYSESLAT, formative assessments and progress monitoring play an important role in your day-to-day work with ELs. To track the progress *Starting* level students—or all your students for that matter—make, take a multidimensional approach. First and foremost, observe the impact of your own verbal and nonverbal behavior for evidence of comprehension and participation. Take periodic anecdotal records on Starting level ELs' participation in instructional activities social interactions and collect student work samples to document how their written expression begins to develop in English.

You will start noticing that Starting level students are bridging over to the next language proficiency level when they begin to communicate verbally and in writing, although their linguistic expressions may be limited to information they are familiar with (including everyday and routine situations). They will begin to use a string of words, memorized phrases, and occasional short sentences. Their receptive skills—how much they understand from what is being spoken or read to them or by them—will exceed their productive language skills, yet you will notice that they begin to ask more questions and seem more eager to interact with peers as well. Look out for Cristela to begin to read at a higher level and become more expressive in speaking and writing. Notice how Tamir is making every effort to explain his projects and describe his artwork using words and phrases that are growing in length and complexity. Remember the memorable phrase from the research of Cook et al. (2008) research—*"lower is faster, higher is slower"*—and anticipate that most of your Starting level students are going to move beyond the early stages of language acquisition with relative ease and speed, and the younger they are, the more so!

Chapter Two

Supporting EMERGING Level English Learners

Who Are *Emerging* Level Students?

Mark and Emilia come from different cultural, linguistic, and academic backgrounds, and they attend different schools at different grade levels, yet they both are labeled as *Emerging* when it comes to their language. As you read about their lives, notice what assets they bring to the classroom and how their teachers could intentionally capitalize on their strengths. Consider what you would do if Mark and Emilia or other students with similar experiences were enrolled in your class and how you would support them with their emerging English language skills.

> A palm tree growing in the shade will not bear ripe fruit.
>
> —AFGHAN PROVERB

Mark

Mark is a fifth-grade student who arrived from China one year ago. It was his first time in the United States and his first experience with the English language. His parents came to the United States five years prior to his arrival to work and set up residency. In the meantime, Mark had been living with his grandmother in Chongqing, one of the largest cities in China, and had limited contact with his parents. When he arrived in the United States without his grandmother, he was angry to have to leave her. Mark and his parents did not know each other very well so the transition was difficult. For much of fourth grade, Mark seemed resistant to learning and communicating with his teachers. He would only speak to other Chinese peers. He often had emotional outbursts, from sadness or anger, which interfered with his learning. One year later, in fifth grade, he shows much improvement and demonstrates English language proficiency at the Emerging level.

He now addresses his teachers and attempts classwork. He participates in small-group work with non-Chinese students, especially when it is well supported with examples, scaffolds, and home language support. During independent work, Mark uses his electronic dictionary and takes great pride in completing tasks with little or no help. He seems to enjoy being challenged, and at times he even asks for additional work. His teacher calls on Mark whenever she is sure he knows the answer. She wants to set him up for success and to give him the confidence he needs to speak in front of the class, which he does more frequently. Since the beginning of the school year, he has been closely watching how other children contribute to large- and small-group discussions and has become a much more active participant in all his core content classes.

→ STOP AND REFLECT ←

Mark had a difficult transitional year after his arrival to the United States and reunion with his parents. What can teachers do to support students in similar situations? In what ways is Mark's current school year a success and what may have contributed to that?

Emilia

Emilia was born in the United States five years ago and is now enrolled in a dual language kindergarten class. Emilia has an older cousin in the same school, who does very well academically. He speaks both Spanish and English with great confidence and fluency, so Emilia's parents wanted Emilia to receive a similar, enrichment-type bilingual education. Prior to entering kindergarten, Emilia was taken care of by family and close friends, who predominantly spoke Spanish to her and read a lot to her in her native language. Although she has lived in the United States from birth, Emilia learned to make sense of the world primarily in Spanish. She was exposed to some English as well, especially through her favorite TV shows and frequent visits to a local playground.

At the onset of the school year, her teachers noticed that Emilia seems to have a weak hand grasp and has a hard time holding anything heavier than a pencil, such as markers or scissors. As a result of early assessment and interventions, she now receives occupational therapy to help her with fine motor skills.

Emilia enjoys spending part of her day speaking and learning in Spanish and part of it in English in her dual language classroom. She seems to be most eager to learn when the lesson centers around storytelling or opportunities for echo-reading, choral responses, chanting, singing, role-playing, and movement. To enhance her skills with letter formation, her teachers allow Emilia to trace letters and shapes in sand, which makes her giggle. Since she enjoys hands-on learning so much, her teachers use a range of creative resources and materials throughout the day as well as iPad apps that encourage her to swipe or tap to get to the correct answers.

→ STOP AND REFLECT ←
Consider Emilia's family background, and determine what assets the family possesses that the school can build upon. What have been Emilia's greatest personal, academic, and familial challenges so far, and how have her teachers been able to address them? What would you do to help Emilia thrive as an English learner if she were in your classroom?

What's in a Name?

The word to describe the second level of language acquisition used in this book and in many other contexts—*Emerging*—is a powerful descriptor. The name suggests that the learner is leaving behind the first stage and moving into a new level of language development: growing in strength and becoming more communicative. The Emerging stage is characterized by students' greater ability to make sense of the world as well to participate in school settings. Students demonstrate a growing level of comfort with the language indicated by consistent signs of emergent language production and evidences of learning.

Keep in mind that English learners (ELs) function at slightly different levels for the four key language domains. Children could have more facility in a certain domain because of familiarity with context, learning preferences, life experience, interest, motivation, and so on. Some might achieve the *Emerging* level in speaking and listening but not in literacy skills (reading and writing). Other students may demonstrate language at the Emerging level in receptive skills (listening and reading) and speaking but not yet in writing. As suggested before, always consider strategies presented in previous as well as forthcoming chapters, rather than strictly referring to this chapter alone.

As you'll see in Figure 2.1, the *Emerging* level of language proficiency has other labels depending on the theoretical framework you refer to, the state or country you live in, or the language development standards you use.

Emerging Level by Other Labels		
TESOL	**Hill and Miller (2014)**	**WIDA**
Emerging	Early production	Emerging

ELPA (2016)	**NYSED**	**California**	**Texas**
Emerging	Emerging	Emerging	Beginner

Figure 2.1

What Can We Learn from Research?

García (2009) introduced the term *Emergent bilinguals* to emphasize rather than ignore ELs' existing language skills and bilingual abilities. In many of her publications she emphasizes that these students function at home and in their communities in their native languages—creating skills, developing new knowledge and understandings. Students bring these abilities and their home languages and literacies to school where they learn to acquire a new language and develop English proficiency. Keep in mind that ELs arrive at school already knowing a great many things that should be valued and leveraged as new skills and knowledge are presented in a new language.

More recently, the concept of translanguaging has taken root, recognizing "linguistic fluidity as the norm" (de los Ríos and Seltzer 2017, 58) for multilingual/EL students. It was originally defined by García (2009) as "an approach to bilingualism that is centered not on languages . . . but on the practices of bilinguals that are readily observable" (45). Further research into this construct reminds us that multilingual students and adults have access to and capitalize on their entire linguistic repertoire constantly, rather than merely communicating in one language at a time, switching back and forth between two separate linguistic entities in their brains. Canagarajah (2013) introduced the idea of translingual orientation to educating ELs by focusing on some key dispositions and perspectives educators should have regarding cross-language approaches in literacy. He suggests that teachers consider "writing and teaching from an awareness that languages are always in contact and complement each other in communication" (4). Based on seminal and current research, it may be concluded that when translanguaging pedagogy is developed based on students' authentic language practices, students are able to draw on their all their linguistic and cultural resources.

What Can *Emerging* Level English Learners Do?

ELs who are recognized to be at the Emerging level of language proficiency represent a spectrum of skills. Some may have just moved along from the Starting level, whereas other may be fast approaching the Developing level.

Students are likely to understand and process a lot more information through listening and reading than they are able to express through speaking and writing. Keep in mind, that there is nothing wrong with English language learners—no deficit to fix. They are whole students we must reach and teach in ways that open their minds to the amazing possibilities of their lives, and language must not be a barrier to that goal (National Education Association 2015, 19).

Continuing with an assets-based philosophy, let's take a closer look at what Emerging level students can do. Notice how successfully and creatively these students can express themselves. See Figures 2.2 and 2.3 for some student work samples by Emerging level students from Victor Honigsfeld's seventh-grade integrated studio and language arts class. See Figures 2.4 and 2.5 for the writing samples that match these elaborate illustrations.

Figure 2.2   Student's Illustration of Her Story About Crossing over a Dangerous Waterfall

Figure 2.3 Student's Illustration of His Story About Comets Colliding with Earth

When it comes to *listening*, you can expect your Emerging level students to begin to show evidence of comprehending what they hear by doing the following:

→ follow one- or two-step directions given by the teacher

→ arrange pictures (photos, illustrations) and objects based on oral descriptions

→ draw or write based on simple oral descriptions or commands

→ understand peer conversation about everyday topics and familiar academic topics

→ understand the main idea of what is being presented but may miss important details or nuances

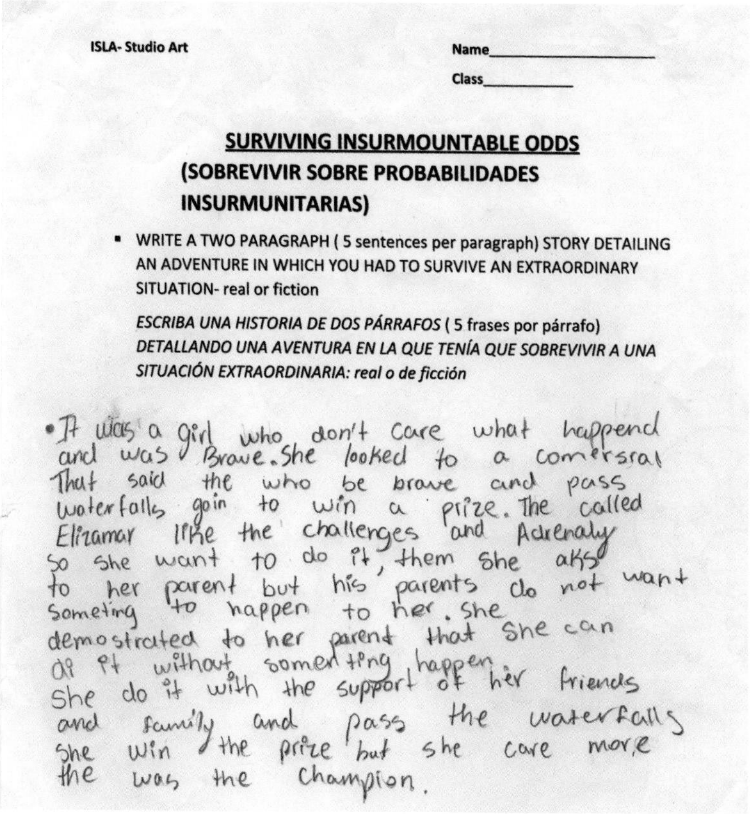

ISLA- Studio Art

Name_____

Class_____

SURVIVING INSURMOUNTABLE ODDS
(SOBREVIVIR SOBRE PROBABILIDADES INSURMUNITARIAS)

- WRITE A TWO PARAGRAPH (5 sentences per paragraph) STORY DETAILING AN ADVENTURE IN WHICH YOU HAD TO SURVIVE AN EXTRAORDINARY SITUATION- real or fiction

    ESCRIBA UNA HISTORIA DE DOS PÁRRAFOS (5 frases por párrafo) DETALLANDO UNA AVENTURA EN LA QUE TENÍA QUE SOBREVIVIR A UNA SITUACIÓN EXTRAORDINARIA: real o de ficción

- It was a girl who don't care what happend and was Brave. She looked to a comersral That said the who be brave and pass waterfalls goin to win a prize. The called Elizamar llike the challenges and Adrenaly so she want to do it, them she aks to her parent but his parents do not want someting to happen to her. She demostrated to her parent that she can do it without somenting happen. She do it with the support of her friends and family and pass the waterfalls she win the prize but she care more the was the Champion.

Figure 2.4 Emerging Level Student's Story About Winning a Prize by Showing Bravery

> → participate in small-group activities by partially relying on what peers are doing while also figuring out meaning by more closely listening

> → construct meaning from spoken words with the help of contextual or visual supports.

Regarding *speaking* skills, you will notice that Emerging level ELs:

> → use memorized phrases and sentences with more confidence

> → share more information about themselves

→ use "incomplete sentences that communicate complete thoughts" (Fairbairn and Jones-Vo 2010, 129)

→ express feelings, preferences (likes and dislikes), and opinions in short phrases and simple sentences

→ ask simple questions about everyday situations and familiar academic content

→ respond to questions with one-word answers, phrases, or short sentences

→ restate what they have heard and understood

→ participate in rhymes, chants, songs, and choral reading more readily

→ describe people and objects using pretaught adjectives

→ describe pictures and illustrations presented to them or prepared by them.

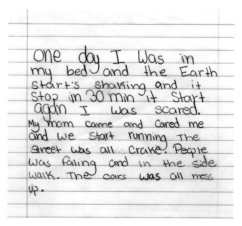

One day I Was in my bed and the Earth start's shaking and it stop in 30 min it Start agan I was scared. My mom came and Cared me and we start running The street was all Crake. People was failing and in the side walk. The cars was all mess up.

Figure 2.5 A Science Fiction Story About a Comet Colliding with Earth

When it comes to *reading,* some younger students at the Emerging level will still be nonreaders in English, yet most are anticipated to develop some foundational skills and increased comprehension. They will:

→ develop basic skills regarding the mechanics of reading

→ understand and retell the main idea of a text, especially if the topic is familiar

→ identify key details, especially if they can continue to use pictures, graphs, and other visual elements for understanding

→ begin to look for text features such as title, subtitle, illustrations, captions, first sentences of each paragraph

→ identify key elements of a story, such as characters and setting.

As far as their *writing* skills are concerned, Emerging level students will:

→ have acquired most of the foundational skills regarding the mechanics of writing

→ continue to label and write single words and phrases using a growing vocabulary

→ continue to illustrate, or combine drawing and writing to express ideas in writing

→ use their native language to communicate (if literate in it) with some English words and phrases included

→ use their native language to help facilitate writing in English, such as brainstorm or outline ideas

→ complete sentence frames that require short phrases

→ produce sentences supported with sentence starters and/ or word banks

→ begin to write sentences independently

→ begin to write short narrative or descriptive pieces

→ write about familiar topics (self, preferences, personal experiences, opinions) and academic topics they have mastered with more confidence

→ make short annotations (such as text markups), as well as take scaffolded or partially completed notes at their reading levels.

See Figures 2.4 and 2.5 for the creative writing samples from the Emerging level students whose artwork was featured in Figures 2.2 and 2.3.

Consider what your expectations are for *Emerging* level students. Just like *Starting* level students, they, too, are most likely to succeed and progress when support is given in multiple ways, languages, and modalities. I expect Mark from the beginning of the chapter to begin to use a range of digital tools for checking understanding (electronic dictionaries), rehearsing his interactions with peers (Flipgrid), and creating digital text (Storyboard). He will be able to communicate with his peers with more confidence using both his home language and growing English skills and also expand his writing into more complete sentences and paragraphs. For Emilia, my expectations are that she will successfully express her ideas by combining drawings and writing words using inventive spelling. She will rapidly increase her oral language skills as she begins to enjoy storytelling, singing, and participating in interactive tasks.

What Practices Support *Emerging* Level Students?

Emerging level students continue to be best supported through teaching practices that are multidimensional linguistically and academically. They need learning activities that allow them to listen to others—both teachers and peers—discuss informal and academic topics. When it comes to contributing to class, Emerging level students need opportunities to share their ideas by expressing themselves not just nonverbally, visually, artistically, and through movement, as Starting level students do, but through expressive language skills as well. Native language use continues to be a critical bridge to acquiring English and being a valued, multilingual student in the class and school community. Figure 2.6 shows a self-portrait created by an English-speaking peer written with the support of Spanish-speaking peers.

When you have Emerging level students in your class, continue to develop their comprehension and involve them in more active language production. Three successful practices to try are (1) targeted vocabulary instruction, (2) verbal scaffolding as adaptive support, and (3) frequent checking for understanding and monitoring comprehension.

Figure 2.6   A Third-Grade English Speaker's Bilingual Self-Portrait

Grow Vocabulary Through Targeted Instruction

Emerging level students will benefit tremendously from the support you give them to grow their vocabulary. The most important tip to keep in mind is that language acquisition is a natural process, so vocabulary has to be integrated throughout the day. Think of your lesson as if it were a story: every story has a beginning, a middle, and an end, and so does every lesson. There are ways to build vocabulary in all three parts of the lesson.

Vocabulary Strategies at the Beginning of the Lesson

Introduce a few, carefully selected words/phrases that the students absolutely need to understand what is coming up in the lesson. Based on the grade-level and content context, choose one or more of these strategies:

→ Use visual supports such as realia (actual objects) and images (illustrations, photographs, pictures, drawings, video clips) to present the word meaning nonverbally.

→ Offer child-friendly definitions or explanations, and, if meaningful, add hand gestures or movements for students to remember the words.

→ If possible, share the native language equivalent for complex concepts.

→ If applicable, break down compound words or multipart words into smaller meaningful units (prefix, root, suffix). Point out the word parts as you introduce the words to help ELs see patterns, such as the prefix *un-* will always mean "not."

There might only be one or two words to introduce at the beginning of the lesson, but phrases and language chunks (words that go together) are also very meaningful as long as they are presented in context and supplemented with visuals or native language support.

Vocabulary Strategies During the Lesson

Revisit the key words/phrases/language chunks you previously introduced. In addition, anticipate what additional words or phrases will be important to the lesson, and pay attention to moments when your students at the Emerging level need clarification or seem lost or confused.

→ Define words when they appear in context, or ask your English-speaking students for help with defining the word, describing the word, or making connections for their classmates.

→ Develop a graphic organizer to reveal connections among words and phrases that may be used across lessons and content areas.

→ Create anchor charts to show the target words in print (with illustrations whenever possible). See Figure 2.7 for Jessica Dribnak's summary of key vocabulary and concepts to help her second graders conduct research on animals and Figure 2.8 for Jill Weatherson's academic vocabulary chart to help ELs develop math vocabulary. Jill and Jessica frequently collaborate and combine their skills and talents to support ELs.

Vocabulary Strategies Toward the End of the Lesson

Take advantage of the last few minutes of your lesson to review the key learnings with all your students but especially with ELs who need opportunities to solidify their conceptual understanding.

→ Connect the target word or phrase to previous experiences in the lesson as you review what the lesson was about.

→ Reinforce the key words by intentionally using them in the closure portion of your lesson.

→ If you use a vocabulary journal to capture key words with Emerging level students, allow them to illustrate their words.

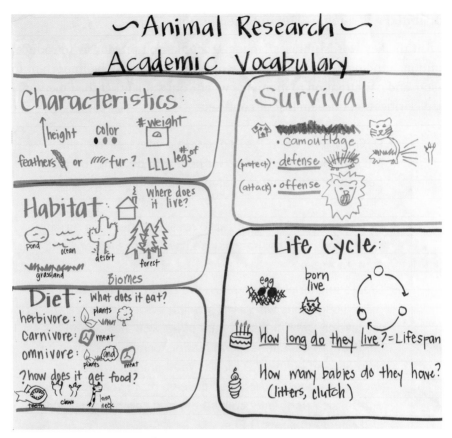

Figure 2.7 Animal Research Academic Vocabulary Chart

Students need to see our own enthusiasm for learning new words so it should span the entire lesson rather than be restricted to, and end up being ineffective, at the beginning of the lesson (Sibold 2011).

Offer Adaptive Verbal Support

Try multiple meaningful ways of presenting material to students and remember to paraphrase and *revoice* students' utterances so they can hear their own ideas in a more academic format, in more complete sentences, and with pronunciation that offers verbal modeling. Pacheco, Daniel, and Pray (2017) remind us to teach in a way that "support not only students' access to new content and language, but also their participation in an activity where using academic language is a valued classroom practice" (63). Let's agree that academic language is not something students *have* or *do not have*; it is something that all students *use* daily to learn at the level and with the tools available to them. Emerging level students are eager to express their ideas, so it is essential to offer adaptive verbal support that includes *modeling, restating,* and *extending academic discourse.*

Modeling

As you speak to your students and describe or explain something, use redundancy and repeat the same ideas in a few different ways, such as in this short excerpt:

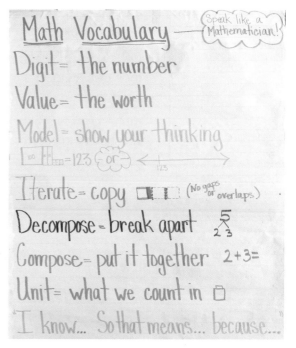

Figure 2.8   Building Math Vocabulary

> Instead of *"Rocks come in different shapes, sizes, and colors,"* try this: *"Rocks come in different shapes. Rocks come in different sizes. Rocks come in different colors."* (Pause and show pictures or real examples of rocks that illustrate the point you are making.)

Model your own thought process by sharing what is going on in your head.

> **"Let me think about it for a moment . . ."** (to show reflection).

> **"What we have discussed so far . . ."** (to show how to summarize).

Restating

> → Try recasting, which is a technical term for repeating what the student said by expanding it and using academic English. (If the student says, "The volcano blows up," acknowledge his observation and recast the

sentence as: "You are right, that picture shows how a volcano erupts").

→ Use synonyms for what ELs have said so they can hear their own ideas in a more sophisticated way.

→ Avoid correcting errors your Emerging level students make, be they grammatical, pronunciation, syntactic, or vocabulary in nature.

Figure 2.9 Oral rehearsal and restating student's ideas also support writing development.

In Figure 2.9, Emily Francis confers with her first-grade student about a short written piece the student is working on in response to the shared reading activity. Emily wants to hear the student talk about his ideas before committing them to paper and helps the student formulate his ideas in more academic ways by restating what the student said.

Extending Student Talk

Teach classroom discourse moves. Prompt students to build on short phrases or sentences by asking, "Can you tell me more about that? That was a really great idea, can you explain it more? What else can you add to that?"

Check for Understanding and Monitor Comprehension

Although all students benefit from frequent monitoring, ELs at the Emerging level of English language proficiency are often at the cusp of understanding what is being presented and discussed, so your vigilance and response to whether they "get" it or not is critical. Teachers are data gatherers and problem solvers, "always shifting the level of scaffolds they provide to balance support with rigor, foster independence, and engage every learner every time" (Singer 2014, 16). When you check for understanding, keep in mind that all learners, especially Emerging level ELs, will demonstrate understanding in multiple ways and multiple modalities, so allow them to show you what they know and can do. The challenge faced by teachers of ELs is not only to gather meaningful formative assessment data and monitor ELs' progress through a range of strategies and tools (see seminal work by Fisher and Frey [2014] and Gottlieb [2016]) but to ensure that students thrive and accumulate new learning by *acting* on feedback they get (Chappuis 2012; Ferriter 2016).

Observations (Look for Nonverbal Signals)

Kid-watching and closer, more carefully planned observations of ELs will provide valuable information (Goodman and Owocki 2002). Watch for nonverbal cues when students do not seem to understand, such as facial expressions, gestures, body language, and restlessness. Use hand signals such as thumbs-up or thumbs-down or one hand–two hands to quickly gather student responses to yes-or-no questions or when students need to indicate their choices between two answers. Try some commonly applied response tools such as erasable whiteboards and color-coded response cards that use the traffic signal to indicate the level of understanding or comfort with the task or topic (green: ready to go, yellow: let's slow down, red: I am at full stop).

Digital Tools for Student Work Sampling

As you observe students engaged in all four domains (listening, speaking, reading, and writing), take advantage of digital tools available for gathering anecdotal records along with authentic written work samples or oral language samples. Notability is one app that allows you to capture your own notes along with photographs of students or their work or even video clips of students' participation. For oral language samples, a simple iPhone, or iPad digital recording will do, or have students digitally record themselves as they explain their ideas or present their work via Flipgrid.

Quick Draw/Quick Write

Use index cards or Post-its for students to quickly respond to a prompt by drawing or writing that reflects their current understanding. A quick-draw

Directions: Choose two work stations. In your own words, explain why you decided that it was a chemical or a physical reaction. Use information from your chart to support your answer.

Station #_____ is a _____

reaction because _____

_____.

Station #_____ is a _____

reaction because _____

_____.

Figure 2.10   Fourth-Grade Science Exit Ticket

or quick-write activity can be embedded at any point in the lesson: to preassess what students know, to check on how they develop new skills and understandings, or as an exit slip, or ticket to leave. Figure 2.10 shows an exit ticket Cynthia Reyes used with her students after a lesson on physical and chemical change.

What Strategies Will Help *Emerging* Level Students Most?

Visual Support

Visual support continues to be paramount for Emerging level students. Although some readily available resources such as pictures, photographs, and video clips will aid in comprehension, intentional, well-planned strategies that build on visual tools will enhance ELs' learning.

Picture Word Inductive Model

The picture word inductive model, or PWIM, is not new to many classrooms (Calhoun 1999; Ferlazzo and Hull-Sypnieski 2018). Its recent resurgence may be attributed to its versatility because it supports visual literacy as well as students who heavily rely on visual modality. In several phases, you elicit words, analyze the words, and help students formulate sentences as they observe and discuss a large picture. They can attach words and phrases to the picture, engage in discussions about it, sort and classify the words they collectively gather, write about the image, and suggest a title that could best describe the picture.

Visual Thinking Strategies

All students benefit from lessons that integrate visual thinking strategies (VTS); however, you will find that Emerging level ELs can successfully develop complex understanding when they learn through visual modalities. VTS was originally designed to engage students in close examination of complex visual texts resembling close reading of textual information (Yenawine 2013). A variety of visual texts can be incorporated into each lesson, as long as the visuals are aligned to the instructional goals, they represent the complex ideas you want to teach, and they help contextualize vocabulary (Capello and Walker 2016). Ask Emerging level ELs to begin by generating a list of what they recognize and can readily identify in the picture; however, it is more engaging and enriching if the image invites students to make predictions and interpret, not just describe, what they see. Claudia Leon adapted the VTS approach to discuss images every Monday based on the lesson plan featured in the *New York Times* (https://www.nytimes.com/column/learning-whats-going-on-in-this-picture). See Figure 2.11 for the anchor chart that guides her students' responses to four guiding questions and Figure 2.12 for how her sixth graders take a first stab at making sense of an image.

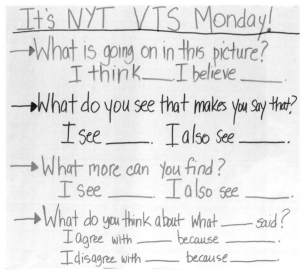

Figure 2.11 Scaffolding Student Responses During a VTS Activity

Learning by Doing

Learning in an authentic manner in real-world context is nothing new. Among many others, Washor and Mojkowski (2013) have made

Figure 2.12 Students independently write about the target image first.

Our Walk Outside

We went outside to look at trees and logs. We <u>saw</u> ants, pill bugs, and rolly polly bugs. We <u>noticed</u> some holes in the logs. We <u>found</u> plants growing on a tree and a log. The log felt soft and spongy. We also noticed pine cones on the ground. Angelica found dandelions. We blew them and we saw the seeds scatter. We loved our walk Outside!

The End.

Figure 2.13 Language Experience Story Based on a Walk Outside the School

a compelling case for increasing student engagement through out-of-school learning experiences. They suggest that "schools must take down the walls that separate the learning that students could do, in school from the learning they do, and could do, outside" (xvii). Firsthand experiences such as visits to local museums, science labs, or animal shelters, or places much further away from home, such as the backstage of a Broadway theatre in New York City or the Smithsonian museums in Washington, DC, not only engage students for the day but may have a life-changing impact. These opportunities undergird the asset-based approach, leveraging life experiences, no matter the language in which they occurred. See Figure 2.13 for how Kimberly Fuller captured a story about a neighborhood walk with her multiage class of first- and second-grade students with interrupted formal education.

Field Trips

Field trips have long been recognized as unique learning experiences for all students (Greene 2016). Recent research has documented that students who saw live theatre demonstrated "enhanced knowledge of the plot and vocabulary in those plays, greater tolerance, and improved ability to read the emotions of others" (Greene et al. 2015, 55). Similarly, students who visit an art museum not only develop more knowledge about art, they also "have stronger critical-thinking skills, exhibit increased historical empathy, display higher levels of tolerance, and have a greater taste for consuming art and culture" (Greene, Kisida, and Bowen 2014, 80). Although visiting live performances and art museums have positive outcomes on all students, Emerging level ELs will gain authentic cultural and linguistic experiences from carefully planned field trips, such as Carol Salva's work with the Texas Historical Commission to create a Heritage Learning unit. Her sixth- to eighth-grade students learned about refugees during the Texas Revolution of 1836. Figure 2.14 shows the replica of an 1832 cabin students visited as a culminating activity.

As a former New York City public school teacher, I took my ELs on five trips that ranged from going on a neighborhood walk and visiting a nearby park to collect fall leaves to more elaborate trips to the Swedish Cottage Marionette Theatre in Central Park (https://cityparksfoundation.org/arts/swedish-cottage-marionette-theatre) and the Queens County Farm Museum (http://www.queensfarm.org). We documented these trips in Photo Big Books, and I found these authentic experiences generated great conversations and led to empowering literacy experiences (Honigsfeld 2009).

Figure 2.14 One of Many Photos Carol Took on the Class Visit to the San Felipe de Austin State Historic Site

Field Trips Without Leaving the School or the Vicinity

Whenever you encounter logistical constraints, consider in-class or in-school authentic learning experiences via guest speakers that should include parent and community volunteers, assemblies, demonstrations, performances, and in-school field trips (see for example http://www.sciencefun.org/schools/ or http://challenge-island.com/programs/school-field-trips/). In Figure 2.15, Brian Wallrapp shows off a tarantula in Connie Goetz's third-grade classroom. Firsthand experience with animals enhances science learning for all.

You don't have to go far to benefit from stepping outside your classroom with the students. Consider taking the class on a tour of the school building and interview the principal, security guard, librarian, or custodian. "Community-based field experiences, such as gardening . . . contextualize and anchor learning" (Reeves and Braun 2012, 105).

Virtual Field Trips

With increasing use of technological tools and Web-based learning opportunities, remember to open up the world to your students through virtual field trips to major historical sites, museums, and galleries from Ellis Island to Anne Frank House, various Smithsonian Museums, Plymouth Colony, and more. Incorporating Google Earth into the experience will allow your students to travel to the destinations you select for your virtual field trip, gliding across states, countries, or continents. Discovery Education (2018) reminds teachers that tours are freely available. You can visit "the National Archives, see how an egg farm works, explore NASA's Goddard Space Flight Center" right from your classroom.

Figure 2.15 A Scientist's Visit

Connecting Real-Life Experiences to Language and Literacy Development

What happens before, during, and after the field trip or other authentic cultural and linguistic experience is over? How you prepare the students for the experience, guide them throughout, and then process and reflect on what students have seen and done are important details to make it a success and to significantly contribute to language and literacy development. See Figure 2.16 for some guidelines on how to maximize the impact of authentic learning experiences.

Oral Language Development

Emerging level ELs are ready for interaction, so position them as thinkers and valuable contributors to the class community. Among others, Roskos, Tabors, and Lenhart (2009) find that "children's speaking and listening skills lead the

Activities Before, During, and After Field Trips	
Before a Field Trip or Other Authentic Experiences	Build up excitement about the forthcoming activity. Generate questions. Have students make predictions. Share similar life experiences students had in another country or context.
During a Field Trip or Other Authentic Experiences	Set up partnership teams (two or three students participating together) to help them engage in authentic conversations and meaningful use of social and academic language. Create a task that helps anchor these authentic learning experiences: have students take digital photos, use a note-catcher template or app to take notes, audio-record their observations, or video-record short examples of the experience.
After a Field Trip or Other Authentic Experiences	Have students dictate a story about their experience and reread the story with you. Use notes, photographs, and digital audio or video recordings to engage in in-class speaking and writing activities: ask students to describe locations and people, recall details, sequence events, or identify similarities and differences of experiences. Create photo essays, class books, posters, or newsletters documenting the experience: have Emerging level ELs identify and label people, places, objects and write captions and fill in thought bubbles and speech bubbles to accompany photographs.

Figure 2.16

Figure 2.17 Fourth Graders Discuss Their Structured Paragraph

way for their reading and writing skills, and together these language skills are the primary tools of the mind for all future learning" (vii). In Figure 2.17 see how Elena Dokshansky's students discuss their work while they refer to a multilingual pocket chart.

Let's keep in mind Emerging level ELs' speaking abilities have to catch up to their thinking abilities, or as Minkel (2018) observes, "A 12-year-old English learner is capable of the same complexity of thought, innovative ideas, and profound questions as a native English speaker of the same age." Universal prompts—as suggested by Bambrick-Santoyo, Settles, and Worrell (2013)—will help facilitate oral language development in all students. The more ELs hear their teachers apply prompts such as "What makes you think that?," "Why do you say so?," and "Why is this important?" to elicit more student talk, the more likely it is that ELs will internalize and use these talk moves with their peers. Jaslyn Davies uses Accountable Talk prompts to engage her students in conversations, which is supported by the anchor chart in Figure 2.18.

One-on-One Time

Giving students undivided attention is difficult, but if you have students engage in learning centers, stations, or independent work, you can find one-on-one time with students. In the early childhood classroom, during center time, a five-minute super-play session allows for undivided attention and interaction with students that give them the opportunity to interact one-on-one with the teacher (Gibbons 2015). In the upper grades, discussing a visual prompt or engaging in a text-based discussion with students will offer targeted modeling of language use. In addition, teacher-led small-group discussions allow for ELs at the Emerging level to benefit from dialogic teaching. In Figure 2.19 see how

Elena Dokshansky conferences with her fourth-grade Emerging level students using a color-coded paragraph writing template from the Step Up to Writing program. Green stands for the topic sentence, yellow represents a key detail or reason, and red offers an example.

Paired Conversations—Peer Interaction

A well-established strategy for student interaction is called think-pair-share (Lyman 1981). First, students receive a prompt related to the topic of instruction. Then they each think about the prompt on their own. Next, they are paired up and share their ideas with their partner. For example, the teacher might ask students to think about all the reasons we should protect endangered animals. Students would first think of as many reasons as they can individually before sharing their reasons with others.

Think-pair-share is one of the most powerful techniques for academic oral language development, especially when this strategy is also connected to reading (Soto 2014). Students can be asked to individually read a selection assigned to them or reflect on a question presented by the teacher, then pair up and share their ideas. Emerging level students can successfully participate when sentence starters or oral language development stems are offered. Zwiers (2018) suggests that teachers

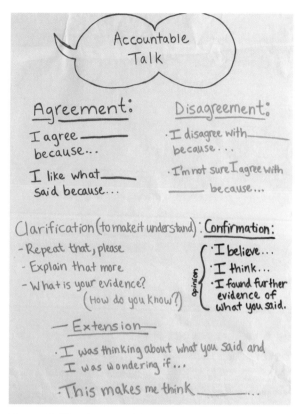

Figure 2.18   Accountable Talk Anchor Chart

Figure 2.19   Writing Conference

Figure 2.20 Think-Pair-Share Planning/
Self-Assessment Checklist

Adapted from http://jeffzwiers.org/fortifying-speaking

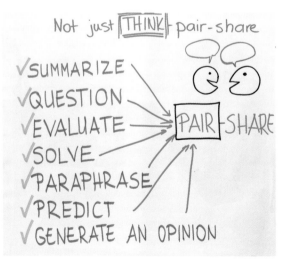

Figure 2.21 Updated Think-Pair-Share

can support the think-pair-share protocol with guided questions as well as a helpful checklist. Tools such as the Planning/Self-Assessment Checklist in Figure 2.20 help structure the activity and offer a framework to observe your students engaged in authentic and meaningful conversations.

Students may become better prepared to share their ideas if you ask them to jot down some key points, thus changing the original *think-pair-share* protocol into *think-jot-pair-share*. Dutro and Kinsella (2010) suggest that "students independently compose a response to a question or task using a response frame or scaffold that guides them in successful use of target vocabulary, sentence structure, grammar and register" (196), thus participating in what they called *think-write-pair-share.* Anderson (2017) pushes beyond the well-established think-pair-share strategy by suggesting that the verb *think* is too vague and it needs to be replaced with other verbs. See Figure 2.21 for an anchor chart inspired by Anderson's work. Use a clothespin or other tool to mark the target strategy.

Triad Talk

As its name suggests, triads go beyond pair work and require the formation of groups of three. Use triads when you group Emerging level ELs during their earlier developmental stage. Preassign groups of three students that will include one Emerging level EL and two other students at higher language proficiency levels. Have them work together multiple times throughout the week for continuity.

The triads provide support as students "rehearse" their responses before sharing out to their whole class. Teach students to include everyone in the conversation by asking each other to add something or clarify their response, to provide evidence to support their claims, or simply to share what they are thinking. See Figure 2.22 for three students working together in Katie Toppel and Molly Haag's cotaught first-grade classroom on a STEM (science, technology, engineering, and mathematics) challenge. While building an igloo, they refer to the Teamwork Talk anchor chart in Figure 2.23 to engage in conversations.

Reading Support

Read-alouds are not just for the early childhood classroom. Students in all grade levels and all proficiency levels benefit from them; yet Emerging level ELs who cannot read on their own (yet) or cannot read with the fluency necessary for comprehension benefit even more! They can be more successfully exposed to literature (both fiction and nonfiction) through read-alouds.

Trelease (2013) reminds us that "we read to children for all the same reasons we talk with children: to reassure, to

Figure 2.22 Engaging in Teamwork with a Shared Purpose

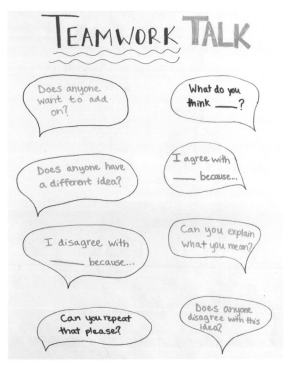

Figure 2.23 Anchor Chart to Remind Students to Use Teamwork Talk

entertain, to bond, to inform or explain, to arouse curiosity, and to inspire" (6). Listening to adults read aloud has a range of positive outcomes for students of all ages, especially for Emerging level ELs.

→ It helps students build receptive vocabulary.

→ It adds to their active vocabulary.

→ It associates reading with a joyful experience.

→ It motivates students to read or explore new topics introduced through the read-aloud.

→ It makes ELs more excited about trying to read on their own (picture walk, skimming, and scanning are all welcome steps by Emerging level ELs).

In addition to helping students with their oral language development, reading aloud to the whole class or smaller groups of children also contributes to building a community of learners and a sense of belonging (Miller 2013). Although interacting with ELs and exposing them daily to conversational English is powerful, Massaro (2017) found that "the complexity of spontaneous spoken language to children pales in comparison to written language in children's picture books" (67). Read-alouds significantly contribute to language acquisition, and they also help students create background knowledge about topics they do not have personal experience with. You can honor ELs' lived experiences if you choose books that reflect their cultural backgrounds. In Figure 2.24, Jill Ayabei is reading aloud to kindergarteners with expression.

Figure 2.24 Reading aloud engages students in predicting the story.

Finally, read-alouds provide Emerging level ELs and their classmates with a reading role model. When a teacher pauses to ask questions or think out loud about the text—also referred to as think-alouds or comprehend-alouds (see Chapter 4)—students develop new appreciation for reading being an active process. When your students have frequent opportunities to listen to you or a more proficient reading buddy read aloud to them, you can count on multiple outcomes: ELs will improve their listening skills, model their own emerging reading skills after you, and emulate your reading behaviors. In Figure 2.25, literary coach Sara Knigge uses a carefully designed planning template for read-alouds in elementary classrooms.

Read-Aloud Tips

→ Ensure all students are seated comfortably, with your ELs seated in full view of you and the book.

→ Show sincere curiosity for the book: if you are excited to read, the feeling will be contagious.

→ Spend some time previewing the book—take a picture walk (for fiction) or text tour (for nonfiction).

→ Read with expression.

→ Adjust the pacing by using clear annunciation, adequate pauses, and lots of facial expression and gestures.

→ Encourage students to create mental images as you read and model how to visualize something by closing your eyes and describing what you see (for Emerging level students sketch out your visualization or share images or photographs).

→ Pause to share your thinking about the text, or invite your students to share their thinking to:

- make predictions
- ask and answer questions
- describe characters
- build theories about the reading
- reflect on the choices a character made.

Title/author/genre
Hook: big ideas/essential questions
Connections to student experience
Connections to previous learning

<table>
<tr><td>

Strategy/strategies focus:

❏ metacognitive: infer, predict, evaluate understanding
❏ summarize
❏ context clues
❏ semantic/graphic organizers
❏ QAR (question-answer relationship)
❏ story/text structure
❏ visualizing
❏ note-taking/highlighting
❏ other

</td><td>

Instruction type:

❏ direct explanation of strategy
❏ model (think aloud)
❏ guided practice
❏ student application of strategy

</td></tr>
</table>

Pages	Essential vocabulary prior to reading (do not spend much time on this)
Pages	**Cognates or tier 2 words to highlight while reading**

Figure 2.25   Read-Aloud Planning Template   Designed by Sara Knigge

Pages	Anticipated areas of confusion

Possible areas ELs need support

Word Level	Sentence Level	Discourse Level	Nonlinguistic
• multiple-meaning words • multiple manners of expressing same idea • sophisticated ways of saying • common words, false cognates • irregular past tense	• passive versus active voice • transitional phrases/ signal phrases • coordinating conjunctions	• imagery • density of academic language • complex sentence structure • dialogue • flashback	• lack of visuals • cultural references • background knowledge

Further reading opportunities with this text

- ❏ shared reading
- ❏ create condensed version for reader's theatre
- ❏ independent reading
- ❏ keyword search and define (drawn, written, Frayer model)
- ❏ favorite page (write or draw and label)
- ❏ create map of setting
- ❏ students are given one teacher-created card of events and the group places the cards in order
- ❏ book review (written, video, trifold)
- ❏ compare to other text on same topic/ same author
- ❏ thought bubble of main character
- ❏ highlight text features
- ❏ create chant with content information
- ❏ create cell phone contacts, messages, apps, texts for main characters
- ❏ Connect Two
- ❏ inside/outside circle for comprehension questions
- ❏ Kahoot, Quizziz, Flipgrid

Figure 2.25

Read-Aloud Extensions

For greater impact, find ways to reread the same text or an extension of the text during guided and independent reading. Read the same complex text aloud again, or even multiple times for different purposes, surrounded by rich conversations. Have students act out parts of the story, participate in role-plays, or use puppetry to enhance engagement and excitement about interacting with complex texts. Place the read-aloud book at a learning center or station so students can reread it or read it to each other while talking about the pictures and retelling what they remember.

Writing Support

When ELs' cultural experiences and existing language skills are maximized, more positive outcomes are expected (Bunch, Kibler, and Pimentel 2014). One way to achieve this is to continue to allow them to use their native languages for brainstorming, drafting, or expressing their ideas in writing. Inviting them to add to their thoughts in English will bridge the languages available to them.

Consider Cummins' (2005) suggestions on how to make meaningful connections between students' native languages and English by applying these strategies:

1. Draw attention to the cognates that exists in the students' native languages and English, thus raising their metalinguistic awareness regarding relationships across languages (as well as awareness about false cognates: not all words that look or sound the same in two languages mean the same).

2. Have students author dual language books by translating from the initial language of writing, such as from their home language to English.

3. Invite multimedia and multilingual projects that honor all the languages the students can use (e.g., iMovies, PowerPoint presentations, Prezis).

4. Initiate "sister class projects where students from different language backgrounds collaborate using two or more languages" (Cummins 2005, 588).

ENGLISH	SPANISH COGNATE	CREOLE COGNATE
physical change	cambio físico	chanjman fizik
chemical change	cambio químico	chanjman chimik
solid	sólido	solid
liquid	líquido	likid
gas	gas	gaz

Figure 2.26 English, Spanish, and Haitian Creole Cognates from a Science Lesson

See Figure 2.26 for a three-way cognate chart from Cynthia Reyes' fourth-grade science class showing key terms in three languages: English, Spanish, and Haitian Creole.

In addition, Velasco and García (2014) recognize that translanguaging may be used in all phases of the writing process, including the planning, drafting, and final production stages. Students can develop bilingual picture books or illustrate bilingual reports to use their full linguistic repertoires as well as visual tools for expression.

Similarly, capitalize on students' ability and willingness to express themselves through nonlinguistic representations, such as allowing ELs to communicate their ideas via drawings, diagrams, or storyboards, or though mixed modalities that integrate written words with illustrations. Digital or traditional scrapbooking encourages student self-expression (Lenters 2016); as students gather textual and visual artifacts around a theme, they can generate a collection of items in a photo album or digital platform such as www.mixbook.com. Invite them to label heavily and write short captions for each item in their scrapbooks. Emerging level ELs will enjoy writing about topics they have more knowledge about and experience with, and they will benefit from writing supports you plan for them. See Figure 2.27 for a seventh grader's sketch note about what he knows about protagonists.

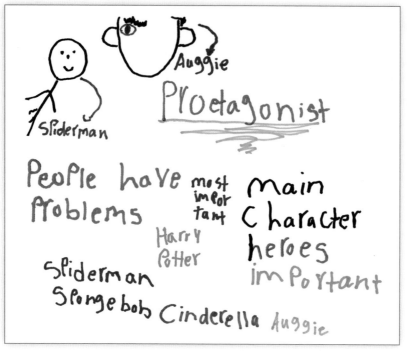

Figure 2.27   Protagonist Sketch Note

Writing Tips for Emerging Level Students

→ Engage students in rich conversations to prepare them for writing.

→ Spend more time on prewriting and shared writing.

→ Structure writing tasks into shorter, more manageable subtasks.

→ Offer step-by-step directions and samples (exemplars or models).

→ Guide student writing with questions and prompts.

→ Offer sentence frames and sentence starters.

→ Supply a word bank or phrase bank.

→ Support writing with visuals, diagrams, or pictures.

→ Confer with students to provide ongoing support and feedback.

In Figure 2.28, see how this student in Katie Toppel and Molly Haag's cotaught first-grade classroom is engaged as he completes a structured writing task about arctic animals, describing what the animals are, what they have, and what they can do. In Figure 2.29, a sixth-grade Emerging level student in Quynh Xayarath's class describes what she is thinking and feeling in contrast to her actions.

Figure 2.28 Writing scaffolds support Emerging level students.

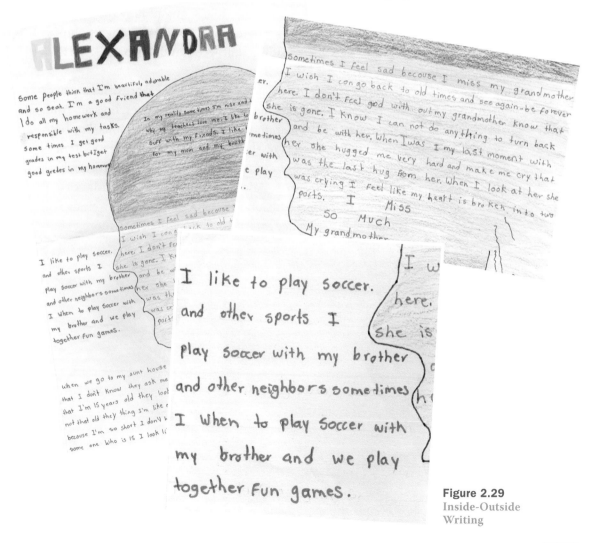

Figure 2.29 Inside-Outside Writing

When Are *Emerging* Level Students Ready to Move On?

Although most schools determine levels of language proficiency and student placement based on annual standardized assessments such as ACCESS by WIDA, ELPA21, and NYSESLAT conducted many months prior (or something like that), formative assessments and progress monitoring play a critical role in your day-to-day, week-to-week, and month-to-month work with ELs. To track the progress Emerging level students make, take a multidimensional approach. Your data collection should include teacher observations of oral language skills (listening and speaking), student work samples to document how their writing skills develop, and reading conferences where you can check on their comprehension and also monitor how their reading skills grow and to what degree they are able to use reading strategies.

You will start to notice that students at the Emerging level are bridging over to the next language proficiency level when you can elicit longer answers from them and observe them participating in more complex conversations. For both Emilia and Mark, single-word answers or short phrases will turn into sentences as they begin to tell more, give some examples, add more details, describe a person or object mentioned, or try to explain their thinking further. Mark's and Emilia's reading fluency and comprehension will increase, and their writing will reveal how phrases and short sentences start fitting together into more extensive forms of expression.

Chapter Three

Supporting

DEVELOPING

Level English Learners

Who Are *Developing* Level Students?

Let's meet Neera and Sergei, two students who are at the *Developing* level of second language acquisition. They have reached the intermediate level in their expressive language skills, yet their academic and social language development requires careful support to ensure success and continued growth. As you read their stories, see if you can relate to their experiences, if you have had students with similar backgrounds and responses to schooling in the United States, and consider what you would do to ensure a successful year for them.

> To learn a language is to have one more window from which to look at the world.
>
> —CHINESE PROVERB

Neera

Neera is a Tibetan student who grew up in India. Her family moved to the United States in the spring of her third-grade year, and she is currently a fourth grader. In India, she received some English instruction as part of her schooling, but in the United States she was classified as an English learner (EL). Neera is a very conscientious student, and it is evident that both she and her family value school and learning. Because Neera has excellent literacy skills in her native language, her English language development has progressed consistently. She enjoys writing and sharing her ideas through writing that she often elaborately illustrates. Neera's teacher uses dialogue journals with her ELs. The dialogue journal, a personalized notebook that is kept at school and is shared only between each student and the teacher, has fostered writing development and relationship building.

A recurring challenge in Neera's writing relates to verb tense. She tends to write in the present tense even when describing something she did in the past. Although she has acquired a sizeable vocabulary, and her writing is comprehensible to the reader, she is cautious when it comes to grammar or sentence structure. She prefers shorter, simpler, well-formed sentences to longer, more grammatically complex structures. Her teachers are working on this through some targeted scaffolding strategies, such as sentence frames and sentence starters. Over the course of a year in U.S. schools, Neera has improved her language abilities in all areas. She actively participates in her stand-alone language development classroom and has surpassed the language skills of some of her EL peers who started out in the same proficiency group as she did.

→ STOP AND REFLECT ←
What were Neera's greatest assets as a new arrival to the United States? What could her steady progress be attributed to? What would you do to help her further expand her language and literacy skills?

Sergei

When Sergei first came to the United States, he was eleven years old. He was identified as a newcomer from the Ukraine, with a strong academic background, fluent in Ukrainian and Russian, with a solid understanding of French but minimal English language proficiency. He was placed in the fifth grade in a suburban neighborhood where his dad accepted a position with an American technology firm. The school provided at least two full periods of language development classes a day to all ELs during their initial phases of language acquisition and home language support whenever possible. Coincidentally, one of the school's instructional aides was originally from Lithuania and spoke Russian, so she was available to translate whenever Sergei's mother came for meetings at the school. She also tried to make Sergei welcome and comfortable in his new school. When she saw him in the hallway or in the lunchroom, she stopped to chat with him in Russian for a few minutes. Although Sergei was reserved at first, he became apt with his electronic dictionary and made friends with two boys, one from India and one born in the United States. The three of them seemed inseparable in the after-school program that offered gaming and coding classes. By the time he finished fifth grade, he made steady progress in English and showed early signs that he would excel in math and science. His mother explained that he was in accelerated STEM (science, technology, engineering, and mathematics) classes back home and really enjoys challenging math problems.

As a sixth grader, he is adjusting to the forty-two-minute block schedule in middle school and not seeing his friends from fifth grade every period. He is a hard-working and serious student, frequently attending the extra-help periods, especially in English and social studies. The pace in some of his core content classes overwhelms him, and there are frequent quizzes, tests, and projects. He continues to do well in math and science and gets by in all his other classes, but he feels frustrated when he cannot express himself with fluency and accuracy. When he gets stuck with schoolwork, he becomes angry with his parents and seems to give up. His content teachers and the English language development (ELD) specialist agreed to meet with the guidance counselor to develop and coordinate a multifaceted intervention.

→ STOP AND REFLECT ←

What are Sergei's challenges? What are his assets that his teachers could tap into? What would you recommend if you were to attend the upcoming team meeting to help him strive in middle school and make continued progress in English?

What's in a Name?

Developing level students are in a unique position. They have reached competence with basic conversational skills; have mastered some essential academic vocabulary; can decode and comprehend high-interest, low-readability texts; and get by using a range of helpful phrases and expressions. With careful scaffolding, ample visual support, and background knowledge about an everyday topic or academic content, they can access and gain a solid understanding of what is presented in class, participate fully, and maintain interest in challenging content. When it comes to expressing themselves orally or in writing, they use words, phrases, and short sentences with increasing confidence; they have yet to *develop* independent facility with more complex academic language and literacy skills, hence the name *Developing*.

An important reminder: as indicated in the previous chapters, be prepared for your students to be at slightly different English language proficiency levels in each of the four key language domains. Some might achieve the *Developing* level in oracy (speaking and listening) but not in literacy skills (reading and writing), whereas others may achieve this level in receptive language skills (listening and reading) but not yet in their productive language skills. So always consider strategies presented across the five proficiency levels rather than strictly referring to this chapter alone.

As you can see in Figure 3.1, the *Developing* level of language proficiency has many other labels depending on the theoretical framework you refer to, the state or country you live in, or the language development standards you use.

Developing Level by Other Labels		
TESOL	**Hill and Miller (2014)**	**WIDA**
Developing	Speech emergence	Developing

ELPA	**New York**	**California**	**Texas**
Progressing	Transitioning	Expanding	Intermediate

Figure 3.1

What Can We Learn from Research?

The zone of proximal development (ZPD) provides an oft-cited framework for understanding the role scaffolding may play in language acquisition (Vygotsky 1978). According to Vygotsky's original definition, the ZPD "is the distance between the actual developmental level as determined by independent problem solving and the level of potential development as determined through problem solving under guidance or in collaboration with more capable peers" (86). The concept of ZPD is well suited for all stages of language development, including the unique situation ELs find themselves on the Developing level: they often have to figure out language use under the guidance of, or in collaboration with, their teachers and peers.

There is a growing body of research exploring the ways ELs may be supported; among them is scaffolding. Bunch, Kibler, and Pimentel (2014) suggest that scaffolding works by envisioning what students will be able to do in the future on their own and responding with the right amount of support offered at the right time. Scaffolding is designed to build independence and autonomy over time (Walqui and Heritage 2012).

An interesting distinction has been made between *macro-scaffolding* (the larger, more comprehensive approach to integrating content and language instruction) and *micro-scaffolding* (the "moment-to-moment work of teaching") (Schleppegrell and O'Halloran 2011, 70) with a focus on offering immediate, readily available support for learners. Walqui (2006) emphatically claims that instead of simplifying the tasks we provide ELs or the language we use in class, "teaching subject matter content to English learners requires amplifying and enriching the linguistic and extralinguistic context, so that students do not get just one opportunity to come to terms with the concepts involved, but in fact may construct their understanding on the basis of multiple clues and perspectives encountered in a variety of class activities" (169).

Research on scaffolding continues to expand. One common takeaway from current research is that scaffolding is not to simplify and reduce content. Its purpose is to offer the amount and type of support when needed and if needed, and eventually to remove the support from the teaching and learning experience. See Figure 3.2 for a scaffolded outline Marisa DeSerio designed to support her sixth-grade students to write an argument piece and Figure 3.3 for a finished essay by a Developing level student.

Persuasive Writing Essay Structure

A) Claim:

Some people think _____ because (**first reason**), (**second reason**), and above all (**third reason**).

B) Body paragraph 1:

a. The first reason why _____ is _____ is **because** . . .
b. For example, (text evidence)
c. This shows or This illustrates . . . (explain how the example fits the claim
d. Then repeat your claim

C) Body paragraph 2:

a. Another reason why _____ is _____ is **because** . . .
b. For example, (text evidence)
c. This shows or This illustrates . . . (explain how the example fits the claim
d. Then repeat your claim

D) Body paragraph 3:

a. The last reason why _____ is _____ is
b. For example, (text evidence)
c. This shows or This illustrates . . . (explain how the example fits the claim
d. Then repeat your claim

E) Conclusion

This shows how _____

Figure 3.2 Essay outlines support writing through structured scaffolding.

Another way to think of scaffolding is to provide students with planning and preparation as well as multiple opportunities to practice oral and written expression, as in Figure 3.4 from Allyson Caudill's, Ashley Blackley's, and John Cox's first- and second-grade classroom. Students prepare for their paired discussions using the color-coded outline and the sequencing links to retell stories. This manipulative effectively keeps students on track with their narratives.

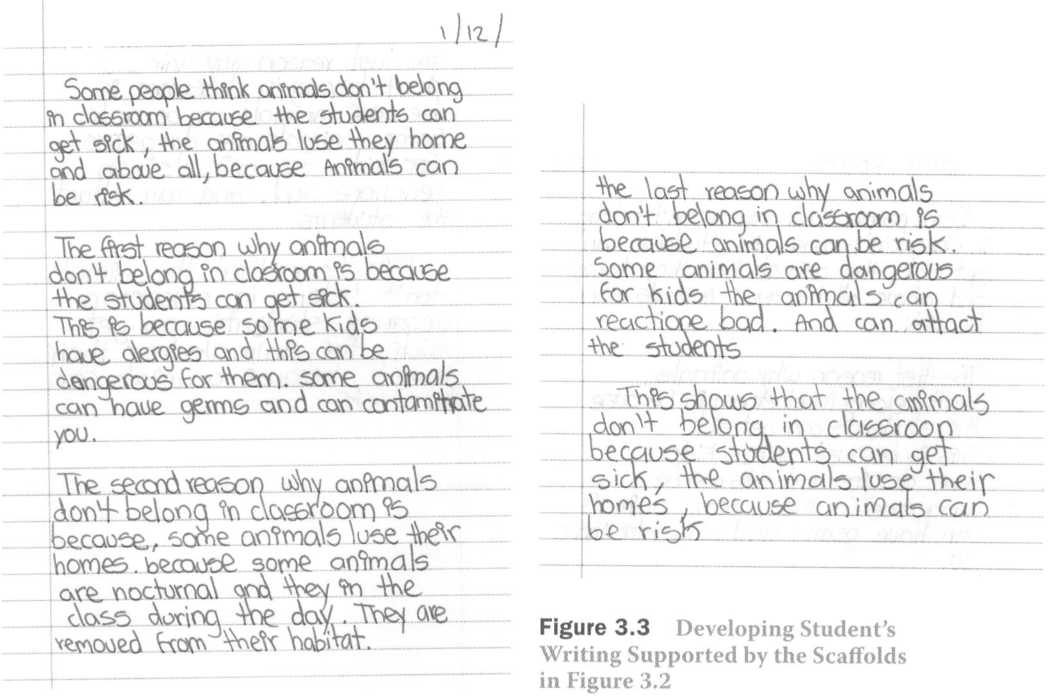

1/12/

Some people think animals don't belong in classroom because the students can get sick, the animals luse they home and above all, because Animals can be risk.

The first reason why animals don't belong in classroom is because the students can get sick. This is because some kids have alergies and this can be dangerous for them. some animals can have germs and can contamihate you.

The second reason why animals don't belong in classroom is because, some animals luse their homes. because some animals are nocturnal and they in the class during the day. They are removed from their habitat.

the last reason why animals don't belong in classroom is because animals can be risk. Some animals are dangerous for kids the animals can reactione bad. And can attact the students

This shows that the animals don't belong in classroom because students can get sick, the animals luse their homes, because animals can be risk

Figure 3.3 Developing Student's Writing Supported by the Scaffolds in Figure 3.2

Figure 3.4
Retell Chain to Support
Sequencing Storytelling

What Can *Developing* Level English Learners Do?

Although there is no set definition of what *developing* means, by and large, your ELs at this level will successfully participate in everyday communicative activities and will be able to converse and read and write about a rage of academic topics using appropriate vocabulary and basic grammatical structures. Let's look at what positive expectations you can have for Developing level students, or as aptly put by WIDA (2012), what these students *can do.*

When it comes to *listening,* you can expect your students at the Developing level to successfully participate in large-group or small-group activities within the following parameters:

→ follow a series of simple instruction

→ follow directions with multiple steps

→ sequence information that is visually supported

→ locate or select key ideas from oral presentations

→ stay engaged in classroom discussions that have a central focus, pretaught vocabulary, and topic familiarity for ELs

→ follow along teacher or student presentations that have ample visual support.

Regarding *speaking* skills, you will find it most rewarding to watch as your Developing level students become more comfortable with English and do the following:

→ participate in everyday conversations and basic academic dialogues

→ use vocabulary needed for everyday communication with increasing confidence

→ express ideas with emerging academic vocabulary (though at times they will be looking for precise words)

→ use simple sentences indicating more and more complex ideas

→ begin to try more extended sentence structures, though errors are common and expected in pronunciation, word choice, sentence structure, grammar

→ respond to questions or prompts with progressively more detail, stringing two or more sentences together

→ become more fluent in conversation

→ retell events in sequence

→ describe people, places, actions, and familiar as well as novel ideas

→ negotiate with their peers in familiar social and academic contexts

→ begin to self-correct.

When it comes to *reading,* students at the Developing level are expected to show a range of skills that expend with focused instruction and sustained opportunities for practice.

→ decode familiar text with increasing fluency (See Figure 3.5 for a third grader in Bethel Aster's class reading with a whisper phone to develop her reading fluency.)

→ read and comprehend *key* ideas in accessible resources

→ demonstrate understanding of what they have read by sequencing events and pictures

→ identify main ideas and key supporting details in a story

→ describe story elements (character, setting, and so on)

→ distinguish text features

→ use context clues to figure out the meaning of words

→ rely on grade-level resources that offer visual or context clues (such as anchor charts, word lists, word boxes, graphic organizers).

Figure 3.5   Reading Fluency Development Supported with a Whisper Phone

Finally, in the area of *writing,* your Developing level students will gain new milestones as they begin to:

→ describe people and places using increasingly varied vocabulary in simple sentences

→ begin to accurately use some content-specific vocabulary

→ produce narratives using shorter (and increasingly more complex) sentences

→ compare and contrast ideas, people, and places

→ produce short expository writing with more and more detail

→ take notes of what is presented orally

→ annotate reading selections with more detail

→ begin to use more complex sentence frames or sentence starters by adding own ideas and words.

See Figure 3.6 for Katie Toppel's fourth-grade student's work, who has reached the Developing level in about a year and a half and is ready to give advice to her peers on how to do well on the upcoming language development assessments. She can formulate complete sentences and, with support, is able to write several simple paragraphs that offer three pieces of advice each! Notice how she consistently uses the sequencing words and how clearly she expresses herself in writing.

Consider your expectations for your *Developing* level students and how they are able to show whether they understand what they hear or read and how they are able to express themselves orally and in writing. My expectation for Neera is that she develops more fluency in speaking and writing. As her teacher, I would challenge her to read, comprehend, and respond to grade-level materials with carefully designed scaffolds in place (see ideas later in this chapter).

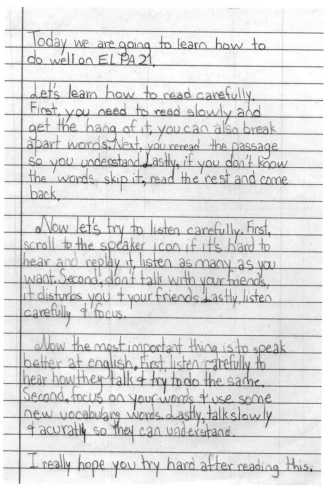

Figure 3.6 Advice from Developing Level Student for Her Peers on How to Do Well on a Test

As a student at the Developing level, Sergei will be able to overcome some of his frustration with the language once he realizes all the things he can already do and how far he has come in a short period time. His teachers and guidance counselor—with an interpreters' help—are in the process of building a personalized, asset-based language development plan that also identifies all the skills he has mastered. I expect Sergei to rely on multiple scaffolding tools that are made available to him when he tries to express himself in speaking or writing.

One strategy I hope he begins to use regularly is to seek out ways to support his own understanding and learning by reaching out to teachers and peers for help before he gets too frustrated.

What Practices Support *Developing* Level Students?

Although the preceding broad-brush descriptions will help understand what your ELs can do, the challenge for you is to create learning activities that not only target and meet students where they are but appropriately challenge them as well. Students at the Developing level will best be supported through helping them expand their vocabulary, engaging them in academic conversations through sentence-level supports, and applying a range of additional scaffolding techniques and adaptations of grade-appropriate texts, assignments, and activities that challenge them and engage them.

When you receive a student at the *Developing* level in your class or when *Emerging* students move to this next stage, be prepared to (1) build tier 2 and tier 3 vocabulary, (2) offer sentence frames and sentence starters, and (3) adapt texts and assignments to make grade-level material accessible.

Build Tier 2 and Tier 3 Vocabulary

Although some vocabulary acquisition strategies may apply both to ELs and their English-speaking peers, others more specifically target ELs. Beck, McKeown, and Kucan (2013) suggest a concise, three-step approach that involves a "thoughtful introduction to a set of words, interesting interactions with the words, and assessments of students' knowledge of the words" (364). These three steps appear to be well aligned to Developing level students' needs since they have an expressed need to build students' vocabulary in a coherent way to enhance comprehension. When adapted to the needs of Developing level ELs, the three steps look slightly different:

> Step 1. Prepare student-friendly explanations for the words that make sense to ELs considering their prior knowledge and experience with the concepts. All the definitions or explanations must include words the students are already familiar with to avoid any further confusion. Photographs, pictures,

sketches, drawings, realia (or real-life objects), short video clips, diagrams, or any other visual support should accompany the words when you introduce them. See Figure 3.7 for an illustrated chart from Carlota Holder's middle school social studies classroom, where she regularly juxtaposes everyday vocabulary (what students say) with academic vocabulary (what textbooks say).

Step 2. Engage students in a range of meaningful activities that allow them to see, hear, and begin to use the words in a variety of ways and in a variety of contexts. Choose from the specific vocabulary strategies that follow to build both tier 2 and tier 3 vocabulary. ELs learn new words when they have multiple meaningful interactions with the target words, with texts where the words appear, and with each other as they make sense of the concepts; use the words independently; and apply them to new situations over multiple days.

Figure 3.7 Illustrated Word Wall That Compares Tier 2 and Tier 3 Vocabulary for the Same or Similar Concepts

Step 3. Use formative assessments to gauge students' understanding as well as productive use of the target language. It's also beneficial to use self-assessment practices such as having students put their thumbs up, sideways, or down to show their levels of understanding for key words. A self-assessment word sort in Figure 3.8 allows students to preassess a set of words the unit will require. For a self-assessment of this nature, make sure you include tier 1, 2, and 3 words that are important for the unit, so students could successfully place words in all three columns.

Based on the comprehensive research review offered by Baker and his colleagues (2014), consider these practical tips along with the rationale behind them:

Target no more than five or six words per lesson for direct instruction. Why? The brain does not hold onto long list of words; instead, a carefully selected group of words presented in context and with lots of supports will go a long way!

Follow the three-step protocol over several days. Why? One-shot deals don't yield retention for vocabulary learning. Language acquisition is like a dance—you take lots of steps in many directions.

Use multiple modalities for vocabulary acquisition. Make sure students hear the words; see them in reading selections, on word walls, in partially completed note-taking pages; and have them write the words, too, through authentic

Words I have heard before	Words I have seen in print	Words I can use on my own

Figure 3.8   Self-Assessment Word Sort

activities. Why? Multiple meaningful encounters with words are needed for them to stick.

Make it functional—focus on phrases and language chunks instead of isolated words. Why? Word lists are decontextualized. When you teach words that go together, they are more likely to be used and internalized.

Use technology to enhance vocabulary learning. Why? There are an increasing number of technological tools and numerous apps available to introduce, practice, and review words, and even to self-assess.

Words will be meaningful for ELs only if they are meaningfully connected to a whole range of other language and literacy learning opportunities that are authentic and meaningful. Nora (2013) cautions against placing too much emphasis on "the acquisition of decontextualized skills such as vocabulary, decoding, and phonics instead of making these skills a part of a larger menu of meaningful activities in a literacy program" (6). In my experience as a multilingual learner and teacher, words will stick so much better if they are personally meaningful, contextualized, and used in multiple ways for multiple purposes.

See Figure 3.9 for an example of the creative ways in which a Developing level student in Alex Wolf's class uses words and phrases to describe herself while also creating a self-portrait. Refer back to Figure 1.30 where a Starting level student's similar work was showcased, and notice the difference in language use.

Figure 3.9 Developing Level Students' Self-Portraits Made out of Descriptive Sentences and Adjectives

Offer Sentence Frames and Sentence Starters

One frequently used strategy to enhance oral communication as well as written responses among ELs is to offer language supports. Scaffolding ELs' Developing language use may be best achieved by providing models, examples, or *partial* models. A sentence starter is just as its name suggests: the first few words of a sentence that give your students a partial model for constructing more complete sentences. A sentence frame often contains the first few words as well as other structural features, such as a verb or additional noun or adjective phrase often found later in the sentence. You are in control of how much of these language frames you will make available and to whom. Some ELs at or beyond the Developing level may find them limiting rather than supportive since they wish to put their ideas in their own words. Encourage that! Cocreate poster-size versions of similar scaffolds with your students to develop even more ownership of this kind of language use, as seen in the cause and effect anchor chart from Quynh Xayarath's eighth-grade classroom in Figure 3.10.

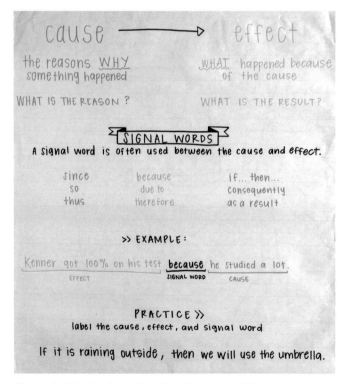

Figure 3.10 Anchor Chart for Cause and Effect

Adapt Texts and Assignments to Make Grade-Level Material Accessible

With increased text complexity, ELs may often find themselves overwhelmed with the density of the text. There are several choices and approaches you can try to ensure they, too, have access to the grade-level curriculum at the instructional (or perhaps even at the independent level) rather than at the frustration level. Regardless of the grade level you teach, think of all the ways that a reading selection can be made more meaningful and accessible by *scaffolding up*. Consider the following list of suggestions for reducing the linguistic demand but *not the academic demand* for ELs:

→ graphic representations (pictures, diagrams, photographs)
→ outlines
→ charts and tables
→ highlighted text
→ key words explained (bilingual, monolingual, or pictorial glossaries).

Figure 3.11a and 3.11b show how an original set of notes (that already supports ELs as they replace dense text with an online format) compares to the adapted version used in Andrea Calabrese and Mike Garguilo's cotaught middle school science classroom.

Topic: Biodiversity

Key Concepts
1. In what ways is biodiversity valuable?
2. What factors affect an area's biodiversity?
3. Which human activities threaten biodiversity?
4. How can biodiversity be protected?

Key Vocabulary

Biodiversity, Keystone species, Gene, Extinction, Endangered species, Habitat destruction, Habitat fragmentation, Poaching, Captive breeding

A. Biodiversity
1. More than 1.5 million species have been identified on Earth.
2. The number of different species in an area is called its biodiversity.

B. The Value of Biodiversity
1. Biodiversity has both economic value and ecological value within an ecosystem.
2. Organisms provide people with food and raw materials for food, clothing, and medicine.
3. Ecotourism has become a valuable resource for many biodiversity areas. Examples: Costa Rica and Belize
4. All species in an ecosystem are connected to one another.

Figure 3.11a Original Science Notes

Topic: BIODIVERSITY (Notes)

Key Concepts	Key Vocabulary
1. Why is biodiversity important? 2. What factors affect biodiversity? 3. Which human activities endanger (=*ponen en peligro*) biodiversity? 4. How can biodiversity be protected?	Biodiversity Keystone species Gene Extinction (extinct) Endangered species Habitat destruction Habitat fragmentation Poaching Captive breeding Pollution Niche Exotic species Native species

A. Biodiversity

1. There are more than 1.5 million species on Earth.
2. **Biodiversity** = the number of **different** species in an area.

B. The Importance of Biodiversity

1. Biodiversity has **economic** and **ecological** importance in an ecosystem.

2. Organisms provide people with food (=*comida*) and materials for clothing (=*ropa*) and medicine.

3. **Ecotourism** is important in many biodiversity areas. Examples: Costa Rica, Galapagos Islands, Belize

4. All species in an ecosystem are **interconnected**.

5. A **keystone species** is a species that **affects the survival** (=*supervivencia*) of many other species in an ecosystem.

   Example: Sea otters are important to control the population of **sea urchins**. Too many (=*demasiados*) sea urchins eat all the **kelp** (plants/producers).

Figure 3.11b   Modified Notes

Andrea Calabrese, middle school English as a second language teacher, explains how she worked with her colleague and the grade-level curriculum to come up with these adaptations:

I highlighted keywords and added supporting images. I also replaced some of the original words with Spanish cognates (for example, value *in the original became* importance *in the modified version). Sentence structure is also simplified (passive voice becomes active voice), and bullet points are used when possible. The use of color in strategic ways (blue = translations, highlighting = key words, red = cognates) also facilitates comprehension*

What Strategies Will Help *Developing* Level Students Most?

Visual Supports

We need to select instructional tools that aid students in both making sense of the lesson to learn new content and skills and building their academic language. Although you can continue to use the visual supports discussed in Chapters 1 and 2, aim for a subtle shift to allow the visuals to serve as supplementary resources rather than as the main vehicle of communication. See summary of tips in Figure 3.12.

See a one-pager in Figure 3.13, which will serve as a partially completed reference sheet on ancient civilizations prepared by Samantha Mallahy for a Developing level sixth grader. This partially completed summary chart invites students to add the missing information.

Learning by Doing

All students benefit from hands-on learning that invites them to explore a topic through experiments or explorations, or by creating or building something collaboratively. The more authentic a task, the more likely students will use language to collaborate and make sense of the task. See Figure 3.14 for an example for planning as school-wide event with eighth-grade students from Quynh Xayarath's classroom.

Tips for Using Visual Support with Developing Level Students	
Kind of Visual Support	**Tip**
Show a two- to three-minute video to preview or review the material	Use www.screen-cast-o-matic.com to create your own videos, and try flipped learning.
Create one-pagers that synthesize all the key information needed for the lesson	Have an advanced EL or English-speaking peer create summary charts to synthesize a unit or chapter for extra credit or service learning credit.
Create partially completed graphic organizers with key ideas already inserted	Use the one-pager you or your students created, and remove some information from it. If needed add a word or phrase box to offer additional scaffold (see Figure 3.13).
Photo projects	Cocreate charts and graphs with your students so they can participate in the process of capturing and illustrating the same information. (See Figure 3.14 for an anchor chart that helps students understand what is expected of them.)

Figure 3.12

Design Experiential or Project-Based Learning Opportunities

Experiential learning opportunities and project-based learning may be supplemental to your teaching or may be central to instruction in your classroom or school. Ayer (2018) suggests four key steps to take for successful projects:

Step 1. Plan with the end in mind.

Step 2. Assist students in developing their own questions.

Step 3. Encourage students to think like experts.

Step 4. Make sure the projects are presented or published for an authentic audience.

Partially Completed Summary Chart on Early River Civilizations

Civilization	Map	Location	Government	Achievements	Geographic Features and Impact
		Middle East Rivers: _____	Sumer = City-States Babylon = Empire		"Fertile Crescent" Silt (fertile soil) = _____
		North Africa River: _____	Kingdoms w/ Pharaohs		Sahara Desert = _____ River = trade and _____
		India Rivers: _____	Unknown Language never translated		Rivers and monsoons = _____ Earthquakes might = _____
		China River: _____	Dynasty w/ Emperor Mandate of Heaven		"China's Sorrow" = flooding Fertile soil = _____ Mountains and deserts = _____

Figure 3.13

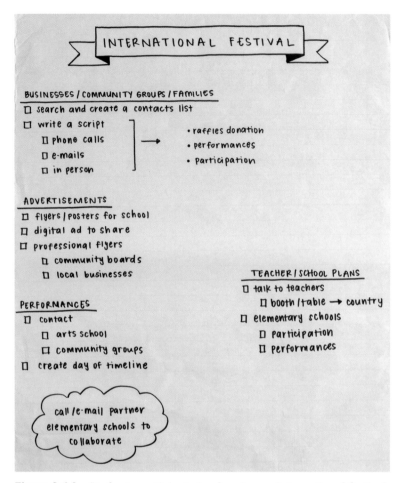

Figure 3.14 Students participate in planning an international festival.

Think of the project or experiential activity as a complex vehicle for academic language and literacy development alongside discovery learning tied to content goals. Three key conditions for experiential or project-based learning ELs to be successful are as follows:

1. Before you begin, analyze the content demand and the linguistic demand of the project you are planning for ELs. Ask yourself these questions:

   • What kind of background knowledge or contextual understanding is required for the project?

- Are there any prerequisite content or linguistic skills my ELs need to work on the project?
- What are some key technical words (tier 3 words) and phrases needed for the project?

2. Create collaborative work groups that ensure active participation by all learners including ELs. Reflect on how to achieve that with these questions:

- How can I strategically place ELs in heterogeneous groups with English-proficient peers as well as other ELs to maximize collaboration and interaction?
- To what extend can ELs effectively also use their native language and literacy skills while working on the project?

3. Scaffold ELs' participation in one or more of the four key language uses (Gottlieb and Castro 2017), and consider how to engage them in all four ways of communicating about their projects and what language frames are needed for ELs to

- *discuss* the project and negotiate all aspects of the group work
- *explain* the purpose and the outcomes of the work the students have engaged in
- *argue* a perspective they had to take during or as a result of the project
- *recount* the key steps taken or essential components of the project.

See Figure 3.15 for an example of a student-created board game from Katie Toppel's fourth-grade ELD class. The students worked collaboratively on an Oregon game board. Not only did the students create the game by adding problems that could occur on the voyage, they also had a chance to practice generating and responding to questions during the game.

Prepare Students for Authentic Presentations

The project becomes more meaningful to students when they present or share it with a real audience. After reviewing what a good presentation looks and sounds like, you can share live or video-recorded model presentations to analyze

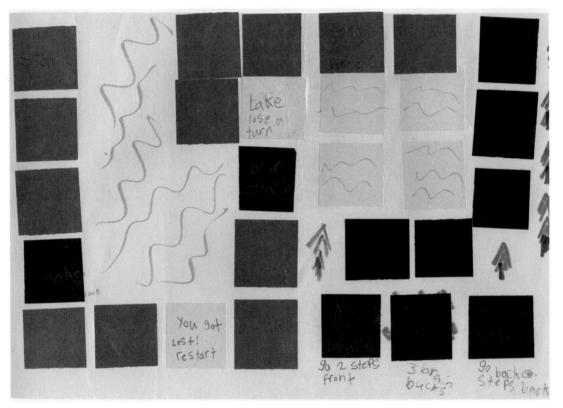

Figure 3.15   Oregon Trail Board Game

and critique. Students will benefit from cocreating a rubric or checklist of the qualities an effective presentation should have. Have teams of students plan and rehearse their presentations to be delivered in person or virtually. A planning guide in Figure 3.16 can further assist students at the Developing level in structuring their presentation.

Oral Language Development

Developing level students will especially benefit from frequent, structured, and purposeful opportunities to interact with their peers and teachers to build their

Our presentation is about _____.

Our audience is _____.

We want my audience to (know, feel, or do) _____

_____.

In the beginning of our presentation, we will _____.

In the middle of our presentation, we will _____.

We will end our presentation by _____.

To make our presentation engaging, we will _____.

Figure 3.16 Group Project Presentation Planning Guide

Adapted from http://www.bie.org/object/document/presentation_plan

expressive and academic language skills as well as encourage risk-taking. Following are some concrete ways to build student confidence:

→ Use flexible groupings strategies.

→ Vary the buddy system or partnerships you set up for ELs to be exposed to and interact with different students for different purposes.

→ Invite ELs to share about their own lived experiences and showcase their in- and out-of-school expertise.

→ Introduce cross-age tutoring.

Reading Support

Since Developing level students will rely heavily on context clues and thrive when working with familiar topics and with other students, reading instruction

for ELs has to consider these learner characteristics. When you differentiate reading selections for ELs, make sure your students are challenged and engaged, like the student in Figure 3.17. Students will be motivated to read if they can choose what they read and have access to high-interest books with lots of visuals.

Figure 3.17 Fifth-Grade Developing Level Student Fully Immersed in Reading About the Tasmanian Devil

Building Background Knowledge

Developing level students may feel lost if the readings are not connected to their prior knowledge of the topic or personal experiences they have encountered so plan on situating all reading instruction in *assessing, activating,* or *building* background first. Review Figure 3.18 for a collection of commonly used strategies for each of the three phases of working with student background knowledge, and see Figure 3.19 for a true-or-false preview sheet Rochelle Verstaendig used with her eighth-grade students.

Guided Reading to Support ELs

In addition to continuously assessing, activating, and building background, engage students in an upgraded guided reading experience that allow for some departure from the three commonly known, yet expandable and adaptable stages. Follow the more traditional protocol, proposed by Temple et al. (2013) and many others.

> *Stage 1: Before Reading*—Introduce and briefly discuss the text selected for instruction with your guided reading group. Use anticipation guides, questions that set the stage for the reading, and other prereading strategies of your choice. The instructional purpose of this stage is for your students to:
>
> - enter the guided reading with curiosity and excitement
> - preview text features or illustrations to get an overall understanding about the upcoming reading

Background Knowledge is Key for Reading Success		
Working with Background Knowledge	**Why?**	**Possible Lessons/Activities**
Assess background knowledge	To find out what they actually know and can already do related to the topic (Don't assume.)	• Freewrites • Brainstorming • Quick draw • KWL • Anticipatory guides • Questionnaires • Alphabet roundups • Think tanks
Activate background knowledge	To bring knowledge and skills needed for the new learning to the forefront	• Personal stories • Picture descriptions • Sequencing • Mind maps • Video clips • Web searches
Build background knowledge	To bridge some gaps you identified through engagement with the first two phases	• Real-life experiences • Field trips • Virtual tours • Guest speakers • Background reading and viewing activities • Hands-on learning • Research experiences

Figure 3.18

- make predictions based on the cover of the book or title of the reading
- ask questions
- use their (activated) prior knowledge to make sense of the new text more effectively
- get hooked at the beginning
- prepare and focus.

Stage 2: During Reading—As your students read the whole text or an excerpt selected for guided instruction with you, observe them for reading strategy use, and offer strategies

What do you know about the government of the United States? Check either true or false after each statement.

	True	False
1. The president of the United States has total control of the government.		
2. All cases that are tried in the United States must come before the Supreme Court.		
3. The legislative branch of the government includes the Senate and the House of Representatives.		
4. If someone believes a law is not allowed by the Constitution, the judicial branch becomes involved.		
5. The executive branch includes the president, vice president, and the cabinet.		
6. The vice president is also the head of the Senate and can vote to break a tie vote.		
7. The legislative branch carries out new laws.		
8. There are currently 100 senators and 435 representatives.		

Figure 3.19 The Three Branches of Government

that promote both their comprehension and critical thinking skills. The instructional purpose of this stage is for your students to:

- read the whole text or a specified selection to themselves either silently or softly whispering
- stop and process what they have read
- select, collect, and organize notes
- engage in a discussion about the reading
- develop new reading skills or enhance existing ones
- employ multiple reading comprehension strategies to make meaning
- request help from you as needed

- make meaning by reacting, responding, and associating
- interact and engage with the text.

Stage 3: After Reading—Engage your students in responding to the reading selection through whole-group discussions, think-pair-share and other paired activities, writing, or acting out aspects of the story. Return to the text, especially the challenging sections of it, to review some reading strategies you used to make sense of the reading. The instructional purpose of this stage is for your students to:

- discuss what they have read
- offer their personal response to the reading and make connections between what they read and what they know
- revisit their predictions and talk about the similarities and differences
- reflect on or explain their strategy use
- synthesize what they have learned and apply the learning in a new way *or* reorganize the information and create something new to internalize and transfer the information.

Writing Support

Writing instruction for Developing level ELs is best conceived as a bridge between oral language development and literacy (Soto 2014). How can your ELs write something that they have never uttered? Ensuring ample prewriting activities that allow for exposure to rich oral language and opportunity for ELs to begin to express themselves in more complex ways is critical to writing growth. Oracy and literacy are intertwined for ELs, and so are skills they already have in their home language and in English. Modeling writing is a complex endeavor for ELs. Think of at least four ways you can employ modeling in the context of writing instruction:

1. **Task modeling:** Explain the expectations and break down the writing task or writing prompt to ensure clarity.

2. **Process modeling:** Show the steps of the writing process to your students.

3. **Product modeling:** Show what the final product may look like so your ELs see the big picture and can better visualize what they will be producing.

4. **Linguistic modeling:** Make explicit connections between how the spoken words you use carry meaning (this is, what we say) and then how it is transferred to a written piece (this is how we write it down) and offer language models.

See Figure 3.20 for a second grader's written work from Michelle Simmonds and Suzanne Malcuit's class. The writing is supported by prewriting activities and through sentence frames, a combination of process and product modeling.

Also see Figure 3.21 for a combination of process and product modeling from Courtney Braese's third-grade class. Jessica Black, her English for speakers

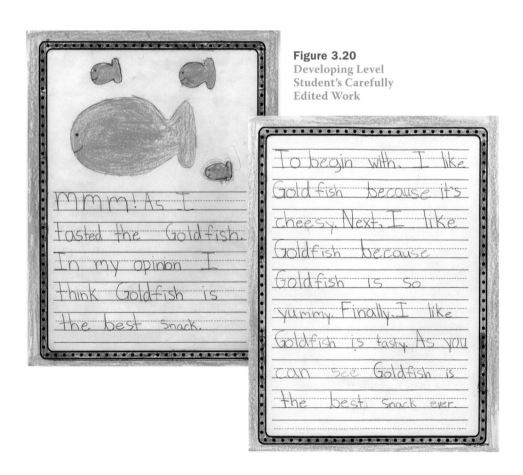

Figure 3.20
Developing Level
Student's Carefully
Edited Work

Poison dart frogs have physical adaptations that help them survive in the rain forest. First, they have toxic skin. This adaptation helps poison dart frogs survive by paralyzing or killing its predators. Poison dart frogs also have brightly colored skin. This adaptation helps them survive by warning predators to stay away.

_____ frogs have physical adaptations that help them survive

in _____. First, they have _____. This adaptation

helps _____ frogs survive by _____.

_____ frogs also have _____. This adaptation helps

them survive by _____.

Figure 3.21 Process and Product Modeling of Constructing a Scientific Paragraph

of other languages specialist colleague, prepared sample paragraphs about poison dart frogs followed by a paragraph frame to scaffold students' writing about other types of frogs using scientific language. Figure 3.22 is a Developing level student's work about glass frogs in response to the scaffolds.

Figure 3.23 shows a color-coded example of how Tonya Schepers and Jennifer Schutte model writing a compare-and-contrast essay for their sixth-grade students.

You can help your students at the Developing level move beyond their earlier accomplishments of labeling, annotating,

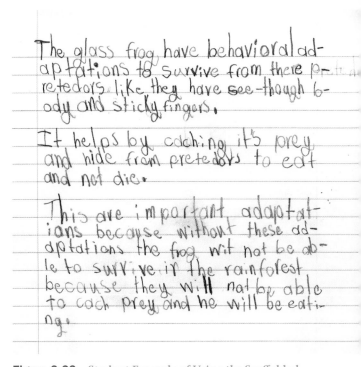

Figure 3.22 Student Example of Using the Scaffolded Outline similar to Figure 3.21

An Incredible Journey

The 2018 release of *A Wrinkle in Time* has been well received by audiences across the United States. It is the most recent theatrical version of the 1962 novel *A Wrinkle in Time* by Madeline L'Engle. **The movie and the book *A Wrinkle in Time* have many similarities and differences.**

There were many **similarities** between the book and the movie *A Wrinkle in Time*. Similar to the movie, the book shows that Meg had to talk to Principal Jenkins. The movie was the same as the book when Charles Wallace tasted the food from the Man with Red Eyes, and it tasted like sand. The movie and the book had Mrs. Who speaking in quotes. Both the book and the movie showed the children on Camazotz bouncing the ball in the rhythm of IT. A final similarity between the book and the movie is that Meg defeated the darkness with love.

There were many **differences** between the book and the movie *A Wrinkle in Time*. In contrast to the movie, the book described a kid on Camazotz who dropped a ball and Calvin, Meg, and Charles Wallace brought it to him. Another difference is that Meg, Calvin, and Charles Wallace used flowers to help them breathe on Uriel, while in the movie, the flowers saved Calvin from falling to his death. Mrs. Whatsit turned into a rainbow-winged centaur creature during the book, while Mrs. Whatsit turned into a giant piece of lettuce during the movie. In the book, Meg, Calvin, and Charles Wallace walked to the city of Camazotz. In the movie, Meg and Calvin were catapulted to the city, while Charles Wallace was waiting for them. Meg and Calvin kissed in the book; however, they did not kiss in the movie.

Both versions of *A Wrinkle in Time* have similarities and differences. Personally, I am always a little apprehensive when books are adapted into movies; however, this movie did a good job hitting all of the key details from the book. Whether it's the movie or the book, everyone should check out *A Wrinkle in Time*.

Figure 3.23 Color-Coded Model Essay

and writing captions and crafting simple sentences and short paragraphs at Starting and Emerging students by:

→ making writing a daily practice through journal writing, where you continue to encourage home language responses alongside English as well as illustrations

→ keeping a dialogue journal, in which you maintain a written dialogue with our students and respond to them in writing (It can be modified to be a peer-to-peer dialogue journal.)

→ engaging them in structured, modeled prewriting activities that activate and build prior knowledge, vocabulary, expressive language chunks about the topic

→ setting up writing buddies or writing teams that allow students to talk about their ideas and may also include shared writing activities (If a Developing level student orally describes a character in the story or gives a recount of the key events, his or her partner or team member may capture these ideas and write them down in a more cohesive language.)

→ engaging in the writing process with ongoing guidance and support (See Lisa Wittek's anchor chart in Figure 3.24 explicitly reminding students what each step of the writing process looks like and what writers are expected to do.)

→ valuing your students' cultural experiences and inviting them to write about what they know and what they feel passionate about

→ offering writing scaffolds: partially completed graphic organizers, note-taking pages, sentence frames, paragraph and essay outlines.

Journal writing is an integral part of Nicole Marino's sixth-grade classroom. She continues to support her students on all levels of language proficiency though multilingual journal prompts (see Figure 3.25).

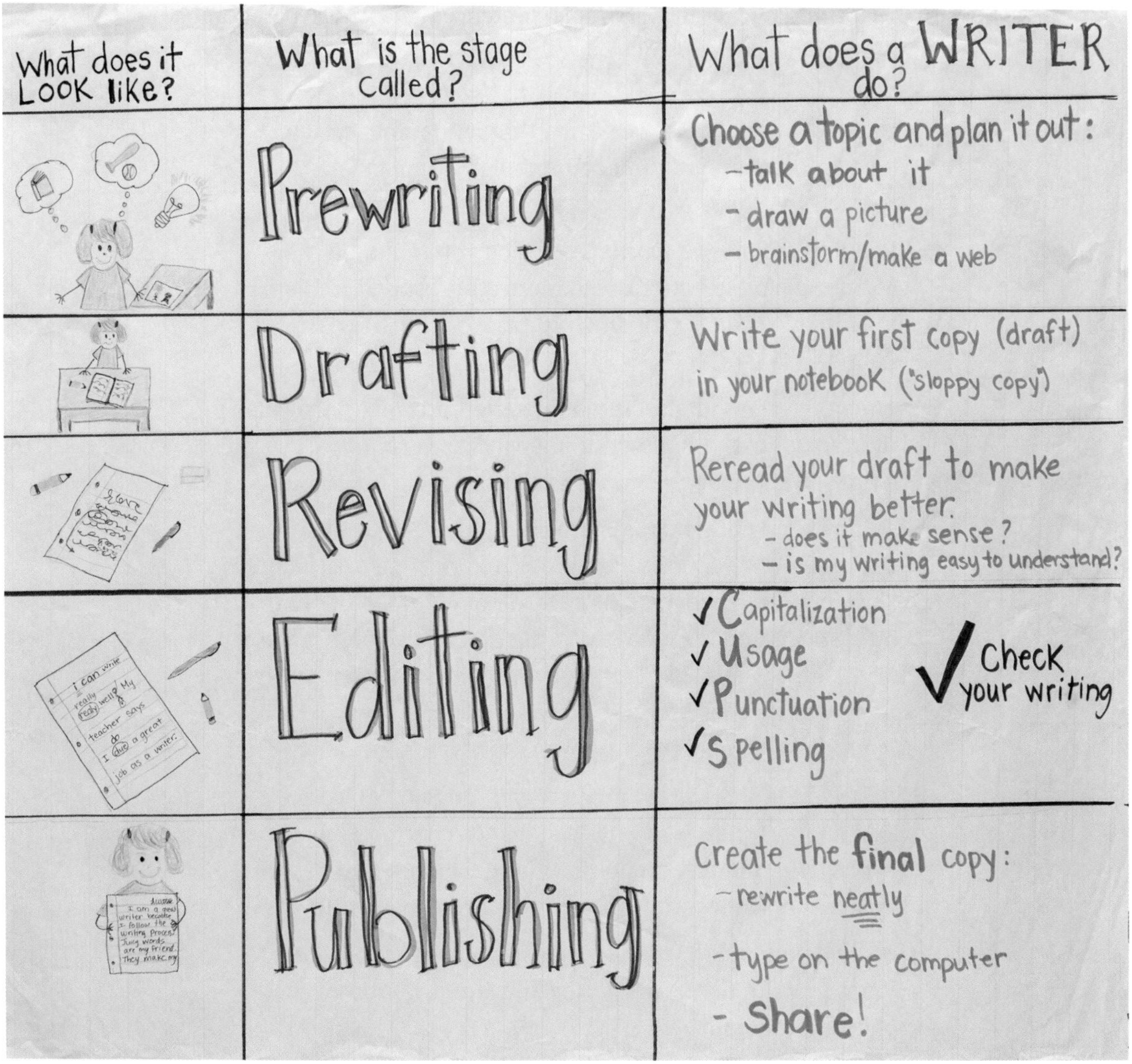

What does it LOOK like?	What is the stage called?	What does a WRITER do?
	Prewriting	Choose a topic and plan it out: – talk about it – draw a picture – brainstorm/make a web
	Drafting	Write your first copy (draft) in your notebook ("sloppy copy")
	Revising	Reread your draft to make your writing better. – does it make sense? – is my writing easy to understand?
	Editing	✓ Capitalization ✓ Usage ✓ Check your writing ✓ Punctuation ✓ Spelling
	Publishing	Create the **final** copy: – rewrite neatly – type on the computer – Share!

Figure 3.24   Writing Process Anchor Chart

Writing Journal

Once a week you will be asked to write a response in a journal. You can write about anything you want, but it must be in your own words (not copied from the Internet!). It has to be at least 5 sentences long. Spelling is NOT important. The most important thing is that we are practicing our writing. You are allowed to write in your home language, and then translate it.

كنكمي .تايموويرتفد يف رد ةباتك عوبسإلا يف ةدحاو ةرم كنم بلطيس سيلو) ةصاخلا كتاملك مدختست نأ بجي نكلو هديرت ءيش يأ نع ةباتكلا تسيل ةئجهتلا .لقألا ىلع لمج 5 درل ا نوكي نأ بجي .(!تنرتنإلا نم خسن كتغلب ةباتكلا كل حمسي .انتباتك سرامن اننأوه ةيمهأ رثكألا ءيشلا .ةمهم .اهتمجرت مث نمو مألا

Une fois par semaine on te demandera d'écrire une réponse dans un journal. Tu peux écrire sur n'importe quoi mais tu dois utiliser tes propres mots pour la réponse (pas de copies d'Internet !). Il faut avoir au moins 5 phrases. L'orthographe n'est pas importante. La chose la plus importante est que nous pratiquons notre écriture. Tu peux écrire dans ta langue maternelle et ensuite traduire.

Una vez por semana se le pedirá que escriba una respuesta de la revista. Usted puede escribir sobre cualquier cosa que desee, pero debe ser con sus propias palabras (no copiado del internet). Debe de ser extenso por lo menos de 5 oraciones. La ortografía no es importante. Lo más importante es que estamos practicando la escritura. Se permite escribir en su lengua materna y luego traducirlo.

Not sure what to write about? Use one of these to help you:

If you could have a superpower, what would it be?	،ةقراخ ةيناسنإ ةردق ىلع لوصحلا كنكمإب ناك اذإ ؟ةردقلا هذه نوكتس اذامف Si tu pouvais avoir un superpouvoir, que serait-il? Si pudieras tener un superpoder, ¿cuál sería?
Where is your favorite place in the world?	؟ملاعلا يف لضفملا كناكم دجوي نيأ Où se trouve ton endroit préféré dans le monde? ¿Dónde está su lugar favorito en el mundo?

Figure 3.25 Multilingual Writing Journal Prompts

When Are *Developing* Level Students Ready to Move On?

Although most schools determine levels of language proficiency and student placement based on annual standardized assessments such as ACCESS by WIDA, ELPA21, and NYSESLAT, formative assessments and progress monitoring play an important role in your day-to-day work with ELs. To track the progress students at the Developing level make, take a multidimensional approach. Your data collection should include teacher observations of oral language skills (listening and speaking), student work samples to document how their writing skills develop, and reading conferences where you can check on their comprehension and also monitor how their reading skills grow and to what degree they are able to use reading strategies. An important and often underutilized dimension of understanding where students are and where they are heading is inviting students to self-assess and to set goals.

You will start noticing that Developing level students are bridging over to the next language proficiency level when they can follow multistep directions with ease and participate in more complex academic conversations in small-group or whole-class settings. They will also use more complex sentence structures that also include more precise academic vocabulary and varied word choice. I expect Neera to understand and summarize the key ideas in grade-level material, and with scaffolds and support, she will discuss increasing amounts of details of what she reads and hears. Sergei is expected to navigate grade-level literature and content area readings and assignments with increased success as well as begin to write increasingly more complex sentences and paragraphs. Both students will begin to demonstrate more independence as a language and literacy learner, though quite differently due to the age difference. With guidance and support, both can learn to accurately self-assess their developing language and literacy skills and set own goals.

Chapter Four

Supporting EXPANDING Level English Learners

Who Are *Expanding* Level Students?

Let's meet Mariana and Youshimi, two students who are at the *Expanding* level of English language acquisition. They come from different backgrounds and attend school at different grade levels, but they have both achieved some important linguistic milestones and have developed an extensive range of skills when communicating both in writing and speaking in English. While reading about their in- and out-of-school experiences, keep in mind the cultural, linguistic, and academic assets they bring to their classes, schools, and larger communities. If you have encountered students with similar backgrounds, how do these stories compare with the ones you know? What experiences and characteristics do these children share, and what is unique about their language and literacy progression? The goal of this chapter is to support expanding ELs' academic, linguistic, and literacy development beyond the Developing level.

The growing millet does not fear the sun.

—ACHOLI PROVERB

Mariana

Mariana is a thirteen-year-old eighth grader originally from Brazil. She came to the United States in fifth grade with some prior exposure to English and strong writing and reading skills in Portuguese. With extended family members already settled in the United States, when she arrived with her family, there was a small apartment waiting for them, along with lots of cousins and friends to help them acclimate. Over the past few years, she demonstrated steady progress in English. She truly enjoys books and reading by herself. While she reads, she uses Google translate to look up unfamiliar words. This process of checking word meaning slows her reading down, but she does not seem to mind. She even takes the time to jot down some of the words she discovers in a pocket-size notebook. She is especially drawn to poetry and historical fiction. Her teachers noticed that she needs well-structured opportunities to engage in dialogue with her peers to develop her speaking skills. Once she feels supported, she participates more frequently, seeking out interactions with her classmates and teachers.

She has shared with her teachers the stories she wrote in Portuguese and expressed her goal to be able to write really well in English as well. She is persistent and will revise the same passage several times until she thinks it's correct. What makes her stand out is that she asks a lot of questions; she even emails her teachers at night or over the weekend. Her curiosity, desire to learn, and willingness to keep trying and asking for help may be one of the secrets to her growth.

→ STOP AND REFLECT ←

What learning strategies has Mariana discovered for herself? In what ways can her teachers further capitalize on these strategies?

Youshimi

Youshimi was eight years old when he left Japan with his parents and younger sister. Youshimi's father is employed by a large corporation and was transferred to the headquarters in the Northeast. When Youshimi arrived midyear, he was placed in third grade and scored at the Developing level in English proficiency.

A year and a half later, Youshimi began fifth grade. There are three other students from Japan, one from Honduras, and one from China in his class along with his English-speaking peers. Although last year he seemed to gravitate toward his Japanese-speaking classmates to clarify some complex assignments or to go over homework after class, in fifth grade, Youshimi is trying hard to be more independent. He is making steady progress learning to communicate in English. He offers elaborate answers to questions about the characters, settings, and plots from stories he reads while occasionally hesitating to consider word choice. He especially enjoys using the apps Book Creator and Storify to make up short stories, which his parents proudly shared with his teachers at the last parent-teacher conference.

Youshimi continues to show improvement in understanding, speaking, reading, and writing in English. Youshimi prefers to choose his own books to read, which are often either much higher or lower than his reading level and driven by his interest in the topic. He has a strong command of simple and compound sentence structures although his transitions and more complex sentences need attention. He has learned to use the Internet to research topics of interest, and he has mastered how to paraphrase and summarize his findings. In one memorable composition, he described the causes and effects of the 2011 tsunami in Japan and even presented his work to his classmates with more confidence than ever before. Right now, his English language development teacher focuses a lot on his public speaking skills and helps him with oral presentations that accompany his Prezis (www.prezi.com), which he prefers to other visual delivery tools such as PowerPoint or Keynote.

→ STOP AND REFLECT ←
Of the many talents Youshimi has demonstrated, which one(s) could his teachers focus on to nurture the most? What type(s) of further support could he benefit from?

What's in a Name?

The term *expanding* suggests that students are in a much fuller command of understanding English, broadening their language and literacy skills, widening their linguistic repertoires, and participating in new and increasingly challenging language experiences every day. The word *expand* comes from the Latin *expandere,* which means "to spread out." If you have previous experience following development of English learners (ELs) across multiple years, you must have marveled at how they begin to spread their wings, ready to soar. There is a word of caution in order: although you might have observed a steady, relatively fast language development from the Starting to the Emerging levels of language proficiency, you might notice that the rate of language acquisition may not be as fast as it was at previous levels. Cook and his colleagues (2008) remind us that "as language learners move to higher levels of proficiency, the rate at which language is acquired slows down" (7). Not only do the complexities of academic language and the linguistic demand of academic tasks begin catch up with the students, you might also notice that catchy phrase *lower is faster, higher is slower* will apply to your students based on their age when they began to learn English and current level of proficiency.

As you can see in Figure 4.1, the *Expanding* level of language proficiency has other labels depending on the theoretical framework you refer to, the state or country you live in, or the language development standards you use.

Expanding Level by Other Labels		
TESOL	**Hill and Miller (2008)**	**WIDA**
Expanding	Intermediate fluency	Expanding

ELPA (2016)	**NYSED**	**California**	**Texas**
Proficient	Expanding	Expanding	Advanced

Figure 4.1

What Can We Learn from Research?

A growing body of research addresses learner agency, learning strategy instruction, and student autonomy, with some very promising work in this field focusing especially on ELs. *Agency* is defined as a person's ability to take an active role in determining what his or her life path would be; on the other hand, *autonomy* refers to one's ability to develop independence and respond to challenges by applying the knowledge and skills he or she has to new situations. Agency and autonomy are two critical characteristics in light of research findings that suggest that "language learners at higher levels of English language proficiency require more time to master linguistic features than lower level language learners" (Cook et al. 2008, 7). It has been established that when students have the opportunity develop metacognitive awareness (thinking about their own thinking), their agency is fostered (Ferlazzo and Hull-Sypnieski 2016). Student autonomy is also evidenced when they understand how they develop new skills and how they can transfer those skills to address new challenges they face.

The importance of strategy instruction is well supported by decades of research by Oxford (2017), who also notes that "deepening strategy instruction to make it more personally valuable for autonomy could be transformative for learners" (2). Helping all students become more self-directed and self-reliant will contribute to their success in and outside your classroom. Although we want to foster independence, interactions are also necessary for language acquisition. Cooperative learning is most powerful after the students have acquired sufficient knowledge and skills to be involved in discussion and learning with peers (Hattie 2012). Others also observe the many benefits of cooperative learning: it promotes active student engagement, contributes to higher peer motivation, and leads to increased achievement (Johnson and Johnson 1999, 2009; Slavin 1995). Cooperative learning also provides a framework for meaningful communication and oral language development. When students interact with their peers and support each other, it has a positive impact both on their academic learning outcome and on socializing into the school culture (Hattie 2012).

What Can *Expanding* Level Students Do?

ELs who are recognized to be at the Expanding level of language proficiency represent a range of language and literacy skills across the four domains. Language acquisition continues to be fluid and dynamic, so expect your ELs to demonstrate different levels of skills in listening, speaking, reading, or writing.

A unique characteristic of Expanding level students is their growing ability to read complex texts for information, to express their ideas in writing and speaking in more precise ways, and to maintain personal and academic conversations by asking clarifying questions, building on their peers' contributions, and explaining their own thinking.

With the asset-based—rather than deficiency-oriented—philosophy adopted for this book, let's look at what positive expectations you can have for Expanding level students, or as aptly put by WIDA (2012), what these students can do.

When it comes to *listening*, you can expect enhanced evidence of comprehending English by Expanding level students. They are likely able to:

→ understand main ideas and most supporting details

→ understand directions but will continue to benefit from visual supports and repetition

→ understand and respond to both everyday and academic conversations

→ process digital recordings (both audio and video) with increased confidence

→ comprehend moderately demanding, contextualized oral presentations.

Regarding *speaking* skills, you will notice that ELs at the Expanding level will:

→ participate in formal and informal conversations with increased confidence and clarity

→ speak comfortably about familiar and academic topics in small- or large-group settings

→ communicate more fluently and spontaneously though some hesitation, self-correction, or rephrasing may be observed

→ use an expanding repertoire of grammatical structures

→ make phonological, syntactic, or semantic errors without interfering with the overall meaning of the communication

→ utilize a variety of words and idiomatic expressions to offer detail about the topic.

When it comes to *reading,* your Expanding level students will demonstrate more complex skills as they begin to:

→ read and understand texts on familiar as well as novel topics with relative speed and fluency

→ read for enjoyment and academic purposes across genres with increased stamina (Lisa Wittek identifies the qualities of each genre with her middle school students; see Figure 4.2 for one example.)

→ comprehend all main ideas and most supporting details in more complex academic texts

→ glean new information by reading texts with clear organization and illustrations but may struggle with dense texts that are written in a more technical language on unfamiliar topics

→ figure out meanings of most words using context clues and prior knowledge

→ continue to find idiomatic expressions and words with multiple meanings challenging.

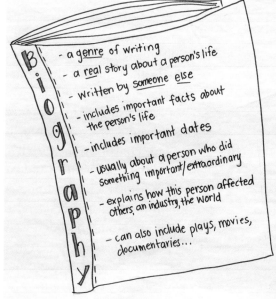

Figure 4.2   Qualities of Biographies Chart

As far as *writing* is concerned, Expanding level students are able to:

→ effectively communicate ideas related to familiar topics (both everyday and academic)

→ write for personal and academic purposes with increasing focus and clarity

→ demonstrate solid control over simple sentence structures

→ experiment with increasingly more complex grammatical structures, but may produce some nonstandard sentences

→ take notes with increasing accuracy and detail based on information they read or listen to

→ write in all major grade-appropriate academic genres (narrative, expository, persuasive) although the lack of discipline-specific vocabulary or complex sentence structures may be occasionally evident

→ with scaffolds and support, organize ideas into logical, well-developed text with occasional errors in word choice, or grammar.

Students at the Expanding level demonstrate increased independence in all four language skills as well as with academic literacy skills. This growth helps them handle the complex linguistic demands they encounter in a variety of academic settings. Mariana, for example, can more easily make sense of texts using various linguistic and technological resources that she learned to harness. She can comfortably and confidently engage in everyday and academic conversations with her classmates, and her writing reflects effective use of sentence structures and paragraph organization with occasional errors that do not distract from understanding her message. Youshimi enjoys independent research projects and reads and writes about grade-appropriate topics that are often presented to him (or he seeks out opportunities to find them) in digital formats. When he participates in large-group discussions, he offers shorter but well-thought-out answers, whereas in small groups, he is more fluent in his expression.

What Practices Support *Expanding* Level Students?

ELs at the Expanding level require experiences that allow them to venture into challenging academic learning with confidence and take risks to express themselves both in writing and speaking with voice and agency. See the confidence with which Rich D'Espositio's second-grade student expresses herself in Figure 4.3 as she sets some new goals for the upcoming year.

When you have Expanding level students in your class, your priority must be to help them become self-directed, independent learners while recognizing that "the observational reality is that second language learners at higher levels of English language proficiency require more time to master linguistic features than lower level language learners" (Cook et al. 2008, 8). Three practices that support Expanding level students are (1) raising metacognitive awareness of their learning process through strategy instruction, (2) metalinguistic skill building, and (3) one-on-one coaching support.

Figure 4.3   Goal Setting for the New Year

Raise Metacognitive Awareness of Their Learning Process

Learners of all ages can develop effective strategies that aid in their social and academic language use as well as continued language development (Oxford 2017). Show students how you self-monitor and self-evaluate language and literacy use, thus fostering metacognitive awareness in students. Remember, you want them to be able to monitor how they use the language, process complex academic content, check their own written work, or reflect on their learning. The following questions provide a plausible place for students to reflect more personally (Fisher, Frey, and Hattie 2016):

> → What am I learning?
>
> → Why am I learning this?
>
> → How will I know that I have learned it?

Self-Assessment Checklist

If your students do not seem to be confident expressing themselves even though they are at higher language proficiency levels, they may need help embracing imperfection. Self-assessment tools, like the one in Figure 4.4 (adapted from Sousa [2011]) can help them understand that making mistakes is a natural part of language acquisition. Figure 4.5 shows Elena Dokshansky's students engaged in self-assessment and peer assessment as a regular part of her class.

Think-Alouds and Comprehend-Alouds

You are likely to continue to read aloud to your students, regardless of their grade level or language proficiency level; you are also likely to think aloud and share your thinking process with them. ELs need insights into your comprehension and meaning-making process when it comes to challenging texts, so make sure you also *comprehend aloud* (Zwiers 2014).

According to Zwiers (2014), think-alouds support the development of a range of reading strategies, whereas comprehend-alouds make visible the processing

Name: _____ **Date:** _____

Learning Experience: _____

	Most of the Time	Some of the Time	Not Yet
Before listening, I gather my thoughts about the topic.			
As I listen, I focus on some key words and phrases.			
As I listen, I ask myself if I have understood all the main points made.			
As I listen, I am satisfied with my level of comprehension.			
After I listened, I think back to how I listened and what I would do differently next time.			

My goals for next time:

Figure 4.4 Self-Assessment Checklist   Adapted from Sousa (2011, 68)

and analyzing of the language of complex texts. See Figure 4.6 for the types of sentence starters you can use to model think-alouds and comprehend-alouds with the text you are reading. Depending on the grade level you teach, these sentence starters may be adapted to match your ELs' readiness levels.

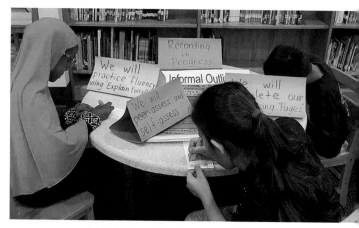

Figure 4.5   Students Engaged in Peer and Self-Assessment

Sentence Starters for Think-Alouds and Comprehend-Alouds

Think-Aloud Sentence Stems	Comprehend-Aloud Sentence Stems
Predicting • When I read the title of the book, I immediately thought of . . . • I predict this story is about . . . • In the next chapter, I think the main character . . . **Clarifying** • I was confused when I read . . . • I had to go back to page . . . • I had to think back to what I learned about . . . **Summarizing** • I think this section is mainly about . . . • The most important point the author is making . . . • So I think the purpose of this article is . . . **Making Connections** • What I just read reminds me of . . . • The section I just read is similar to . . . • When I read this section, I thought of . . . • I think the author wants me to . . .	**Word or Phrase Level** • I noticed that the author uses the same word here . . . • I am not sure what this word means in the first paragraph, so I will reread this section . . . • I have never heard this word before. Let me see if I can figure out the meaning by reading ahead/looking for some examples/finding an illustration. • The author begins the sentence with the phrase . . . **Sentence or Text Level** • The author uses a very long sentence in this paragraph. Let me see if I can break it down into shorter sections, such as . . . • In this section, I noticed some sentences are have a similar pattern to . . . • I noticed this section has a lot of dialogue and quotes. I wonder . . .

Figure 4.6

Adapted from Dodge and Honigsfeld (2014)

Reading Checklist

To enhance text-level comprehension, Afflerbach and colleagues (2013) recommend that teachers model questions that foster metacognition including reading with a purpose, meaning making, and anticipating and solving challenges encountered while reading. Some questions to consider are, Why am I reading this text? Does this passage make sense? If not, where is the problem? Can I fix the problem I encounter, and what strategies will I be using? See Figure 4.7 for a metacognitive checklist for reading that can further help students become reflective readers and learners.

Build Metalinguistic Skills

Expanding level students are steadily growing their simple sentences into more complex ones. This growth happens through ongoing opportunities to participate in authentic, collaborative, inquiry-based conversations that enhance stu-

Name: _____ Date: _____			
What I am reading: _____			
	Most of the Time	**Some of the Time**	**Not Yet**
In general, I have a goal in mind before I begin to read.			
As I read, I remember why I am reading.			
As I read, I focus on understanding the text.			
When I read, I keep an eye out for problems.			
If I feel there is a problem while I am reading, I try to identify it.			
I try to fix the problems I find while I am reading.			
I try to maintain my reading, even when I encounter problems.			
My goals for next time:			

Figure 4.7 Metacognitive Checklist for Reading   Adapted from Afflerbach et al. (2013)

dents' expressive language. As students engage in meaningful dialogue, they are more likely to string together multiple sentences and take risks with more complex sentence structures.

ELs also benefit from brief, guided explorations of carefully selected complex sentences directly embedded in the lesson. This practice, also called *sentence dissection* (Dove and Honigsfeld 2013) or *sentence cross-examination* (Dodge and Honigsfeld 2014), is best accomplished if the excerpt comes from a text used for literacy or content-based instruction, such as a textbook or a piece of literature. See Figure 4.8 for a visual breakdown of a target sentence (Pearson 2016) and Figure 4.9 for a summary table on how to help unpack the sentence so it could serve as mentor text.

Although the sample sentence in Figure 4.8 is seemingly simple and easy to process, the complexity comes from working with longer chunks of language.

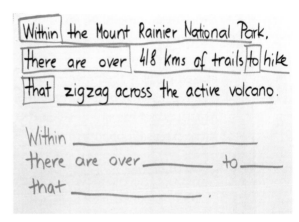

Figure 4.8 Cross-Examination Example

Guiding Questions for Sentence-Level Work	
Guiding Questions and Prompts for Meaning	**Guiding Questions and Prompts for Form and Usage**
• What is the sentence about? • Let's look on the map to see Mount Rainier National Park is. • Let's click on the Mount Rainier National Park's website. Based on these pictures how would you describe it? • How long is 418 kilometers? • What does *trails* mean in this sentence? • What do living things depend on? • Why do living things depend on their environments?	• Form a circle with your hands as if you were holding a big ball and say "within." The author begins the sentence with this word within. What's another way we can say the same? • When the author says "over 418 kilometers," do you think he means "over there" or "more than"? Let's try to use that phrase in a new sentence: *There are over 500 students in this school = more than 500 students.* • The author uses a special word, *zigzag*. Let's try to act it out, what does that hike look like?

Figure 4.9

Cross-examining complex sentences builds not only ELs' receptive skills and metalinguistic awareness, but productive language skills as well. The sentences you spend some time on also serve as mentor texts that invite students to generate sentences of their own with similar structures. When you present a sentence frame generated based on the mentor sentence, students add their voices and experiences to it and develop ownership of complex sentence structures. See these extension opportunities:

> *Within New York City, there are over one hundred museums to visit.*

> *In this movie theater, there are over ten movies to see.*

Provide One-on-One Coaching

Expanding level students may present as fluent, confident conversationalists and may also read and write close to grade-level proficiency. Yet, you might find that some students in this group of ELs may also hit a plateau or experience decelerated progress compared with their previous learning trajectory. One-on-one coaching will help students to clarify their thinking and polish academic language use. Katherine Lameras regularly takes the time to confer with her students individually while the rest of the class is engaged in partner work or independent work. In Figure 4.10, Katherine makes sure her student takes notes about what she is learning.

Although one-one-one conferencing is extremely beneficial for all students, your coaching should serve a multidimensional purpose of supporting independence and autonomy, a *take charge and keep trying* attitude, as well as language and literacy development skills and concept attainment. Coaching may be scheduled regularly or occur spontaneously to review or reinforce what the students know and do well as self-directed learners. According to Barber and Foord (2014), coaching ELs offers them support through motivation, organization, and practice. When you coach Expanding level ELs, take into consideration the guidelines in Figure 4.11.

Figure 4.10 One-on-one coaching supports Expanding level ELs with targeted interventions and guidance.

Coaching Guidelines		
Guidelines for Conferring	**How to Do That**	**What That Sounds Like**
Always use a strength-based rather than deficit-based approach to coaching.	Build on areas that students excel at, and name their strengths with precision (what the students already know and are able to do well).	"Excellent use of '_____,' our new word from today's lesson! I am looking forward to seeing or hearing you use that word again!"
Help students set periodic goals to develop independence and foster self-monitoring.	Create a weekly or biweekly plan with learning goals codeveloped with students, and have them track their own progress.	"This week, let's continue working on how you use verbs in your sentences when you edit your own writing. What specific goal would you like to set for yourself, and how will you keep track?"
Guide students to take responsibility for their own learning and progress.	In addition to setting goals, have students identify ways they can reach them and reflect on what they have already accomplished.	"I know your goal is to come to school prepared every day, especially having your homework done. You have done much better these past two weeks than at the beginning of the year. Can you tell me what you did differently?" "Let's go over your plan to meet your goal of having homework done every day. "
With upper elementary and middle school students, focus on study skills, organizational skills, and some other non-academic skills that students need to overcome day-to-day in-school challenges.	Have them keep a learning log with periodic reflections on how they tackle assignments and various learning experiences.	"Your learning log has lots of entries that talk about your reading habits. I really enjoyed reading about how you could not put your book down one night and were reading under the cover using your iPhone as a flashlight. I would love to see how you feel about the readings assigned by your teachers."
Help students see themselves as experts, as scientists, as historians, as readers, and as writers.	Coach them to think, read, and write like a scientist or historian by specifically focusing on the type of academic language that is associated with each field.	"When you work on your report, remember how scientists organize their information. Do you think written notes or diagrams would help you better plan your paper?"

Figure 4.11

Take the time to get to know your Expanding level students, and, as their coach, ask lots of questions, gather information about their progress, and listen closely to their ideas. And then, remember to celebrate them!

What Strategies Will Help *Expanding* Level Students Most?

Visual Support

Although visual support is essential in earlier stages of language development, it continues to be helpful for all learners. Multisensory experiences or multimodal input may no longer replace verbal input, yet it enhances cohesion and meaning making.

Graphic Organizers

Instruction across all grade levels and content areas may be well supported with graphic organizers that help outline:

> → what the students already know (try variations of the KWL [What I know; what I wonder; what I learned] chart)
>
> → what they anticipate will happen in the story (set up an anticipation guide)
>
> → what concepts are developed in the piece (develop concept maps).

Story maps, character webs, time lines, and many other graphic organizers that match the genre and complexity of the target text or task will help ELs synthesize their learning.

A common recommendation is to use a small set of graphic organizers consistently to help Starting or Emerging ELs have access to complex core content or to see connections between ideas, concepts, words, and phrases, such as a well-tested set of graphic organizers including T-charts or Venn diagrams. Expanding level ELs, however, will benefit from more complex visual representations to enhance their cognitive processing skills and receptive and productive language skills. Tonya Schepers' graphic organizer in Figure 4.12 challenges her eighth-grade ELs' thinking since they represent complex concepts, complex relationships between ideas, or more complex visual representations.

Planning Organizer for Creative Writing

Directions: Use this graphic organizer to plan out your amazing short story.

Synopsis: What is your short story about?

Narrator

- Who is this person?
- What will their voice be?
- What is their point of view?

Characters

Name: Age: Physical details: Conflict: Contribution:	Name: Age: Physical details: Conflict: Contribution:	Name: Age: Physical details: Conflict: Contribution:
Name: Age: Physical details: Conflict: Contribution:	Name: Age: Physical details: Conflict: Contribution:	Name: Age: Physical details: Conflict: Contribution:

Figure 4.12   Planning Organizer for Creative Writing

Created by Tony Schepers

(continues)

Planning Organizer for Creative Writing, *continued*

Conflict(s)
- What will the central struggles be in your story?

Theme(s)
- What are the central messages of your story?

Symbols
- What meaningful objects will you incorporate into your story?

Plot

Exposition: • • • •
Rising Action: • • • •
Climax: • • • •
Falling Action: • • • •
Resolution: • • • •

Figure 4.12 *Continued*

Thinking Maps®

If you are looking for a consistent or systematic way of supporting ELs' thinking, explore Thinking Maps (www.thinkingmaps.com). With proper training, Thinking Maps are implemented throughout whole schools to create a common visual language for teachers, students, and administrators. Each map is specific to certain thinking processes, thus the cognitive and metacognitive processes are concisely connected to eight visuals, each with its own protocol. Figure 4.13 summarizes the key purpose of each of the eight Thinking Maps and offers lesson ideas on how to apply them to K–8 literacy and core content instruction for ELs. Figure 4.14 shows an anchor chart that Kayla Cook and her EL specialist colleague Alejandra Howell use to explain one Thinking Map (Tree Map) to their first graders.

Thinking Map Summary Table		
Kind of Thinking Map	**Purpose**	**Examples from K–8 Literacy and Core Content Lessons**
Circle Map	Define in context (adding a frame of reference)	• Create a frame of reference for rules within the classroom, school, or larger community. • Brainstorm about good learning habits within the context of the grade level.
Tree Map	Classification	• Classify various clothing articles according to the four seasons. • Summarize the achievements of the Maya Civilization.
Bubble Map	Description	• Describe the main character of a story. • Describe the characteristics of a simple machine.

Figure 4.13

Thinking Maps® is a registered trademark of Thinking Maps, Inc.

(continues)

Thinking Map Summary Table

Kind of Thinking Map	Purpose	Examples from K–8 Literacy and Core Content Lessons
Double Bubble Map	Comparison and contrast	• Compare and contrast two main characters in the story. • Compare two geographic locations.
Flow Map	Sequence or order of events	• Describe the steps taken in a science experiment. • Describe the key events in a story.
Multi-Flow Map	Cause and effect	• Discuss the events that led to the Declaration of Independence and the events that followed it. • Explore the causes and the effects of climate change.
Brace Map	Part-whole relationships	• Identify the major systems of the human body and the organs found in each system. • Identify all the oceans and continents. • Name parts of an insect.
Bridge Map	Analogies	• Explore the relationship between part and whole, change in size or age, or antonyms and synonyms.

Figure 4.13 *Continued*

Learning by Doing

To foster independence and study skills, have students create their own learning tools, using both traditional materials (such as paper and pen) and digital resources. In the process of making an instructional tool, Expanding level ELs will have opportunities to use their creativity and internalize what they are learning while also developing independence.

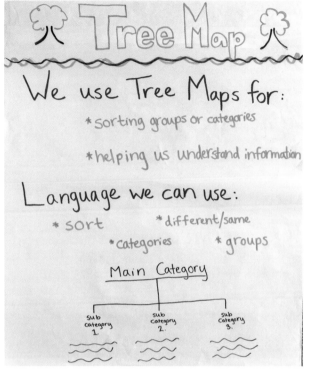

Figure 4.14 Explicitly Teaching How to Use Tree Maps

Foldables

When it comes to student-created instructional materials, the possibilities are endless. One hands-on tool is foldables. Foldables, popularized by Dinah Zike (1992, 2012), are three-dimensional graphic organizers that are devised by cutting and folding eight-by-eleven-inch (or smaller) sheets of plain or colored paper for students to organize written information.

Foldables can be used to help retell a story, describe a character, show a cause-and-effect relationship, note a problem and its solution, illustrate the sequence of events, or record main ideas and details. The focus is not so much on being creative, although it often helps reluctant writers to participate. Since foldables can be used in any grade or content class and can be differentiated and scaffolded to match students' readiness and interest levels, they also serve as independently developed study tools. See Figure 4.15 for Amy Eckelmann's first grader working on his foldable about adjectives.

Digital Tools

A variety of digital tools allow students to create digital content and use them to practice, internalize, share, or demonstrate new learning. Students can work alone or with peers to research and create presentations with some

Figure 4.15 First grader makes a foldable about adjectives.

commonly used tools such as Power-Point or Prezi, or you can help students venture into more versatile tools such as creating an e-book or a ScreenChomp presentation, both of which incorporate audio recordings, videos, a range of different visuals, and texts. See Figure 4.16 for a summary of key digital tools that students can learn to use independently (Parris, Estrada, and Honigsfeld 2016) and Figure 4.17 for Michelle Gill's third-grade student using Green Screen by Do Ink to prepare a presentation about an animal she researched.

Digital Tools and Their Main Impacts on Student Language and Literacy Development		
Digital Tool Type	**Examples**	**What Can Students Do?**
Productivity tools	Evernote, Notability	Take notes and organize ideas using new technology
Social learning platforms	Edmodo, Google Classroom, Edublogs, ePals	Write and produce digital content for authentic audience
Multimedia presentations	ScreenChomp, Prezi	Read books with patterned language or introduce a sentence frame and use a word wall to scaffold student writing.
Language and literacy-building tools	Book Creator, EDpuzzle, Nearpod, Explain Everything, ShowMe, Learn-Zillion, Discovery Education	Listen, read, view, and process through multiple modalities at their own rate of acquisition
Information-sharing tools	QR codes	Participate in or create scavenger hunts; share online resources
Formative assessment tools	Quizlet, Socrative, Kahoot!, Knowmia	Show their understanding and participate in new learning through gamelike activities

Figure 4.16

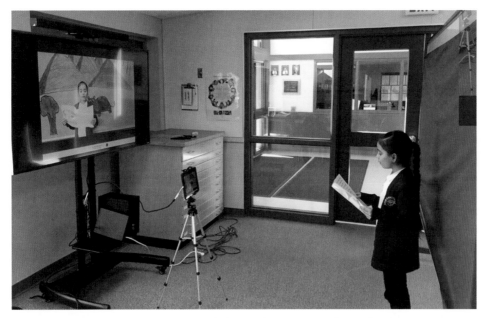

Figure 4.17 Green Screen by Do Ink helps students express themselves in creative ways.

Oral Language Development

It has been frequently cited that the classroom is the place for the much-needed "social occasions that provide opportunities for discussants to think, speak, listen, and learn together, with and across their differences, about a specified topic" (Parker 2006, 11). The emphasis is on *across differences*! It is not just students at the Expanding level who benefit from cooperative or collaborative learning; in fact, it is most effective if students engage in classroom talk across proficiency levels, languages, and cultural backgrounds. See Anjali Sengupta's first-grade students work together to choose a shape, observe it, write their observations, and help each other complete a summary task in Figure 4.18.

Figure 4.18 Student collaboration supports team learning.

Both researchers and educators whose work is informed by sociocultural theory embrace collaborative processes for learning. Johnson and Johnson (1999), Slavin (1995), and others have found cooperative learning to lead to stronger peer motivation, active student engagement, and increased achievement while also providing opportunities for meaningful communication and oral language development (McGroarty 1993). Although there are many cooperative learning strategies, such as four corners, line up and fold, stand up-hand up-pair up, and send a problem, here I offer some specific details about two: jigsaw and carousel.

Jigsaw

Students start in heterogenous *home groups* of three to five members. The team will work on a complex assignment, as the name of the strategy suggests, like putting the pieces of a jigsaw puzzle together. Each student will focus on a different aspect of the assignment, such as read a different passage or paragraph, complete a different subtask, or become specialized in a subtopic. Students leave their home groups to work with members from other groups who are assigned the same subtopic, reading, or task in their *expert groups*. After mastering the material or completing the task, students return to their home group and take turns sharing with their original group members what they have learned and "piece together" through shared learning. See Figure 4.19 for an example of four expert group tasks developed based on the picture book *Tulip Sees America* by Cynthia Rylant (adapted from Yahya and Huie [2002]).

Carousel

Students work in small groups of three or four to explore a topic at the beginning of a unit to activate and build prior knowledge or at the end of the unit to review and synthesize new learning. Start by setting up one sheet of chart paper per group around the room with different questions, problems, or quotes related to the lesson. See Figure 4.20 for sample carousel rotation questions/prompts for a social studies unit in second grade and a science unit in sixth grade. Notice the predicable and repetitive sentence structure in each.

Give each group different-color markers to use, or give each child his or her own maker for more individual participation. Students move around the room in rotation with about one to two minutes to discuss the question at each station and to jot down their ideas. Remind them to read the questions carefully

Expert Group Tasks

Expert Group 1—Map Readers You will use a map of the United States to follow Tulip's trip. When you return to your home groups, you will help the members of your group track Tulip's trip across the United States. (Bonus task: Write out the list of the states Tulip crossed, and find their capitals.)

Expert Group 2—Illustrators Your task is to create matching picture and word cards from the story for each verb and then to categorize them by state. (Bonus task: Write a sentence using each word and act out the following action verbs: *flap*, *bark*, and *swim*.)

Expert Group 3—Project Organizers You will orally sequence the story and then retell it in sequence to your home group. Use a Flow Map to take notes and organize key details (Bonus task: Create your own graphic organizer about the story.)

Expert Group 4—Poetic Language Detectives You will be the poetic language detectives and authors of your home groups. You will identify and explain all the similes in the story. (Bonus task: Write some additional similes that the author could have used to describe the beauties of the American landscape.)

Figure 4.19 Jigsaw Activity Using *Tulip Sees America*

Planning Grid for Carousel Questions/Prompts

Second-Grade Social Studies Example on Urban/Suburban/Rural Areas	Sixth-Grade Science Example Related to Living Organisms
It is great to live in an urban area because _____.	Why are producers important in an ecosystem, and what are some examples?
It is great to live in a suburban area because _____.	Why are consumers important in an ecosystem, and what are some examples?
It is great to live in a rural area because _____.	Why are scavengers important in an ecosystem, and what are some examples?
	Why are decomposers important in an ecosystem, and what are some examples?

Figure 4.20

and check the previous answers written by other groups before they contribute theirs. Keep the groups rotating around the room to answer all the questions on the chart paper. Gray (2016) recommends the use of a timer, a brisk pace, and a closure that generates a whole-group discussion.

Reading Support

The kind of reading support Expanding level ELs need is very similar to what all learners benefit from. Two ideas for supporting ELs with expanding their reading skills: (1) text engineering that transform texts that represent grade-level complexity into more accessible passages, and (2) a summary of close reading strategies that include text annotations and word-, sentence-, and text-level questions on three levels of complexity.

Text Engineering

The idea of adapted texts for ELs has been around for a long time. For too long, the adaptations focused on simplifying the text in a way that the original richness of the ideas and grammatical structures and text features were largely removed, thus denying ELs to explore text complexity. Billings and Walqui (n.d.) suggest an approach that represents the best of both worlds: retaining the rich, complex message of grade-level texts while ensuring deep interaction with passages that are modified in several ways. I interpret this approach as capturing the key features of a read-aloud and inserting the following elements into a revised/adapted text:

1. Add guiding questions to set a focus for reading.
2. Insert additional subheadings without giving away too much.
3. Chunk the text into smaller, more manageable passages.
4. Add linguistic redundancy by repeating names of people or places instead of replacing them with pronouns.
5. Add visuals with captions that support conceptual or contextual understanding.
6. Leave a wider margin around the text for student notes and text annotations.

See Figure 4.21 for how fourth-grade teacher Harry Baumander used text engineering to explain data from an article the class read about pizza consumption. Harry did his research and found images of every key item referenced in the short passage: the 1.2-mile pizza complete with the oven, the three major types of pizzas, and a 103-year-old photograph of the first pizzeria in New York. Students also learned that an average American eats over 6,000 slices.

Close Reading: Annotating and Questioning on Three Levels

When you plan close reading for ELs, consider a short but rich selection of about 200–250 words. Although close reading can be and ultimately will be completed independently, initially choose teacher-led explorations for ELs at the Expanding level. Look for culturally relevant and engaging texts since students will be reading the text multiple times: they need to stay enthusiastic and interested in the material. During the first reading, have students read for general understanding and for personal reactions. During the second, have students annotate the text, a technique that will need to be modeled and explicitly taught to ELs. See Figure 4.22 for text annotation reminders.

Step 1: What does 6,000 look like? How can we make the number 6,000 come alive?

Step 2: See the diagram below in which each triangle consists of 100 smaller triangles. Therefore, 60 × 100 = 6,000 triangles represent the amount of pizza eaten during the person's lifetime.

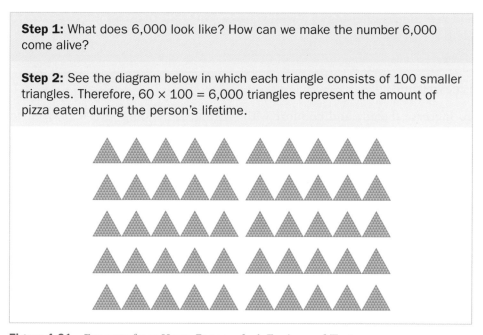

Figure 4.21 Excerpts from Harry Baumander's Engineered Text

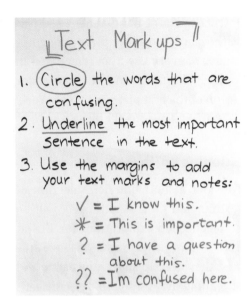

Figure 4.22   Text Annotation Anchor Chart

During the subsequent readings, have students answer increasingly more complex questions that address word-, sentence-, and text-level understanding as shown in Figure 4.23. The goal is to move students from concrete, foundational questions first to ones that integrate text comprehension with language features and their own thinking, and then to abstract and complex questions for critical analysis.

Writing Support

Students at the Expanding level of proficiency need opportunities to negotiate meaning in multiple different ways across different content areas. One challenge they need to face—and they are definitely up to it with your guidance—is to use writing *as a tool to learn* across the content areas.

Freewriting

To increase fluency and comfort with writing, Expanding level ELs need to write, and write a lot, without the fear of being corrected. Since mistakes are inevitable, some ELs at this level, especially upper elementary or middle school students, may become self-conscious and hesitate to deviate from examples or models offered.

Illustrated Notebooks

Illustrated notebooks are designed to pose questions and answer them through multiple modalities. Students use verbal or pictorial or mixed notes from the text they read, teacher presentations, videos, or other resources. Their notes may include drawings, diagrams, connections, key words, or information organized in a new way. Additional printed resources maybe cut and pasted into the

	Questions to Support Close Reading		
	Concrete, Foundational, and Factual Questions	**Questions That Integrate Language, Thinking, and Text**	**Abstract and Complex Questions for Critical Analysis**
Text level	What is the title of this reading? Look at the headings and subheadings: What do you infer/predict about the reading based on those text features? Look at the illustration on page X. What details stand out in the illustrations?	What is the main purpose of this author? What evidence is there that shows _____? Why did the illustrator choose to offer details on _____? How are those details also depicted in the text?	What is the theme of this story? What message is the author trying to give the readers? What is the central idea or underlying message of the text? How does this story compare to another story we have read? How can you justify your answers?
Sentence level	Which sentence introduces the topic? Which sentence identifies _____? Which sentence describes _____?	Which phrase or sentence helps the reader understand what the author means by saying _____? Can you find examples of where the author _____?	The text begins with _____. Why do you think the author chose to begin the text this way? The text ends with _____. Why do you think the author chose to end the text this way?
Word level	What is the first important word in this text? What does the word _____ mean in this text?	What words does the author use to convince the reader about _____?	What words stand out as carrying the most important piece of information? Why did the author choose the word _____ to describe _____?

Figure 4.23

notebook, as well as highlighters and different-color pens and pencils, can add visual enhancements to presenting and organizing information (Honigsfeld and Dodge 2015). See Figure 4.24 for how Harry Baumander demonstrates the use of interesting words to enhance his students' writing and Figure 4.25 for a page from a kindergartener's illustrated notebook from Emily Francis' class.

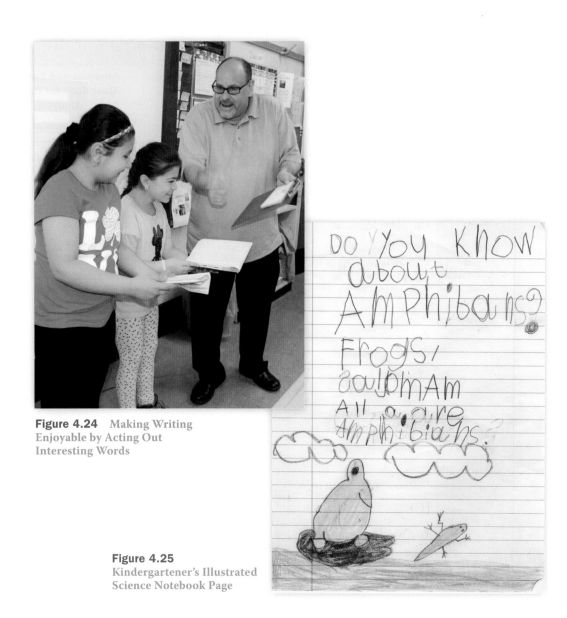

Figure 4.24 Making Writing
Enjoyable by Acting Out
Interesting Words

Figure 4.25
Kindergartener's Illustrated
Science Notebook Page

Scaffolded Note-Taking

To help students learn how to participate independently in lessons that are based
on observations and explorations, scaffolding provides the necessary support.
See Figure 4.26 for Dana Moccio's scaffolded note-taking sheet for her eighth-
grade science class.

Scaffolded Note-Taking to Support Writing a Lab Report

Problem: How is a light stick affected by thermal (heat) energy?

Hypothesis: A. If we place the light stick in hot water, then _____

_____,

because _____

B. If we place the light stick in cold water, then _____

_____,

because _____

Procedure

1. Observe the **unbroken** light sticks, and record your observations in the data table.
2. Bend the other two light sticks until the ampules break. Record what happens in the data table.
3. Place one broken light stick in the ice water, and one broken light stick in the hot water.

Record your observations in the data table.

DATA TABLE

Light Stick	Observations	Describe Brightness of Light Stick
Unbroken light stick at room temperature		
Light stick in cold water		
Light stick in hot water		

Analysis and Conclusion

1. **How** did the amount of light energy released from the light sticks **differ** in the hot and cold water?

   _____

   _____

2. **Explain why** the different temperatures (hot and cold) affected the amount of **light energy** released.

   When we added thermal energy (hot water), the light stick glowed _____

   because _____.

   When we removed thermal energy (cold water), the light stick glowed _____

   because _____

Figure 4.26   Scaffolded Note-Taking to Support Writing a Lab Report

Created by Dana Moccio

When Are *Expanding* Level Students Ready to Move On?

Although most schools determine levels of language proficiency and student placement based on annual standardized assessments such as ACCESS by WIDA, ELPA21, and NYSESLAT, formative assessments and progress monitoring play an important role in your day-to-day work with ELs. To track the progress Expanding level students make, take a multidimensional approach. Your data collection should include teacher observations of oral language skills and student work samples to document how their writing skills have developed and reading conferences where you can check on their comprehension and also monitor how their reading skills grow and to what extent they are able to apply reading strategies.

You will start noticing that Expanding level students are bridging over to the next language proficiency level, which is referred to as Bridging—no pun intended—when they can observe higher levels of fluency and accuracy in reading and speaking and more extended responses to questions posed orally or in writing. See Figure 4.27 for Courtney Braese and Jessica Black's third-grade student's finished story about pollywogs. It is written in the pourquoi tradition as an origin story and requires advanced writing skills to explain why pollywogs want to become frogs.

Thinking back to the two students introduced at the beginning of the chapter, I expect that Mariana will understand not just the main ideas and important supporting details but some subtle nuances when she listens to others. She will use varied, increasingly grammatically complex and longer sentences in speaking and

---

Why do polliwogs want to become frogs?

Long, long, long ago in a park there lived a polliwog named Annie. Today it was a summer day and Annie was about to go to the pool.

Annie was very nice and extremely shy. She had small eyes and small legs, a small mouth, and a small body and always enjoyed swimming.

One day Annie was on her way to the park where water is because she needed to learn how to swim. Then Annie was scared to swim. After swimming Annie felt happy and thought that she can swim. Then she became a frog.

Later on Annie went to go swimming and thought about she can swim for a long time. Then she said that she was not scared to swim. And decided she was happy to become to become a frog.

The next day Annie realized that she became a frog. And so that is way, for this day, all polliwogs always want to become a frog so they can swim without being scared.

Figure 4.27 Origin Story About Pollywogs

writing and produce more complex texts as well. You will notice that Youshimi understands digital recordings (both audio and video) and participates in face-to-face oral interactions with more confidence. He will use multiple reading strategies independently to tackle grade-level texts though occasionally will need some scaffolds. His written work will reflect logical organization and fewer, less significant errors in word choices or grammatical structures.

Chapter Five

Supporting

BRIDGING

Level English Learners

Who Are *Bridging* Level Students?

Let's meet Jetta and Francis, two students who are at the Bridging level of second language acquisition. As with all other students in this book, they, too, come from different cultural, linguistic, and academic backgrounds and attend school at different grade levels. They have developed an extensive range of skills when communicating both in writing and speaking in English. The goal of this chapter is to help figure that out and offer some insights into supporting students who have reached near-native fluency.

> Knowledge is a treasure, but practice is the key to it.
>
> —ARABIAN PROVERB

Jetta

Jetta is a second grader, currently at the Bridging level of language proficiency. Jetta came from the Philippines when she was in kindergarten and has two older siblings who are close in age and also reached high levels of language proficiency within a few years. Her mom speaks multiple languages and dialects. Although she is not comfortable holding a conversation with teachers in English, she seems to understand everything. Jetta's father always comes along to meetings; he speaks and understands English well and takes great pride in his three daughters' academic progress in the United States.

Jetta has had a strong command of conversation skills in English since she entered school. In kindergarten, she couldn't describe some of the pictures used during instruction, especially if they had anything to do with urban contexts. At times she would forget some words when she lacked a solid frame of reference. However, she quickly learned foundational literacy skills, and by the end of first grade she was reading alongside her English speakers in her classroom. When she began second grade, her teachers noticed that most activities and lessons do not have to be adapted for Jetta. In fact, her teachers began to challenge her and regularly included her in enrichment groups such as solving complex math problems, working on creative writing assignments, and participating in maker education sessions (https://makered.org/about/what-is-maker education/).

As a second-grade student, Jetta is in a reading group that is slightly above her English-learning peers. She is excited to read and talk about chapter books. She relates to characters and often makes connections to her own life and experiences. Her teachers are focusing on getting Jetta to engage with complex texts and slow down her reading to ask herself higher-order questions.

→ STOP AND REFLECT ←

What strategies could Jetta's teachers use to help her with deeper understanding of complex text? How can they use her creative strengths to improve in areas of literacy?

Francis

Francis is a sixth grader from the Democratic Republic of Congo. He came to the United States speaking three languages: French, the official language of his country and the language in which he received his education so far; Swahili, one of the most common national languages; and some English he picked up when his father was a visiting scholar in Nigeria for a year.

At this point Francis presents as a multilingual speaker, at the Bridging level of English proficiency. He is one of very few students his teachers have ever seen who can translate confidently among three languages, English, French, and Swahili. His teachers often look at him in amazement and affectionately call him a sponge. When he was a new arrival three and a half years ago, he tested at the Developing level of proficiency, and his teachers immediately noticed how much he loved to take risks and experiment with English. Whenever he was unsure of a word in English, he "anglicized his French words," which meant he tried to say French words he knew with an accentuated English accent. Although it worked many times, at others times it led to some confusion or even laughter. Francis heartily laughed along at his attempts and explained his strategy, "It's French, I know, but it almost sounds like English, so why not try?" He participates in class discussions and has lots of friends. His social personality coupled with exceptional oral language skills makes it easy to recognize Francis as an outstanding student. Yet, he needs continued support with academic writing. He likes to explain his thoughts and elaborate orally but is a reluctant writer. When he does commit to writing a more extensive piece, his writing reads the way he speaks. His core subject teachers and his English language development specialist have agreed to approach this challenge in an interdisciplinary, collaborative fashion. They incorporate short, frequent writing tasks that build his disciplinary literacy skills and use more formal, academic word choices and sentence structures as well as multipart assignments that build up to more elaborate, longer pieces.

→ STOP AND REFLECT ←

What assets does Francis bring to the class and school that could be further utilized? How can his strengths be used to address the challenges he is facing with writing?

What's in a Name?

Language proficiency levels are never static. Your students may reach Bridging level in some domains such as oral language skills as they are able to maintain conversations with near-native or native-like fluency or read with confidence and deep understanding. At the same time, they may continue to experience challenges in one or more other domains, such as having difficulties organizing ideas using an expository genre. Figure 5.1 shows that the *Bridging* level of language proficiency has other labels depending on the theoretical framework you refer to, the state or country you live in, or the language development standards you use.

The name suggests that the students are reaching an advanced level of proficiency that is often comparable to their monolingual peers. Keep in mind that, as lifelong learners, they will not just be done with English acquisition once they test proficient and may no longer receive specialized instruction or services in English language development. Instead, they will continue to need support and ample opportunities to expand their language skills. Haynes and Zacarian (2010) suggest that teachers "identify student gaps in listening, speaking, reading, and writing, and deliver lessons that are specifically geared toward closing the gaps "(114).

Similar to Figure 4.1 in the previous chapter, this chart, too, seems to suggest a close alignment. Most frameworks recognize that students at this level

Bridging Level by Other Labels		
TESOL	**Hill and Miller (2014)**	**WIDA**
Bridging	Advanced fluency	Bridging

ELPA (2016)	**NYSED**	**California**	**Texas**
Proficient	Commanding	Bridging	Advanced high

Figure 5.1

are at an advanced level of language development, metaphorically conjuring up the image of a bridge that connects these students to full competency with the language.

What Can We Learn from Research?

In a recent publication, Valdés, Poza, and Brooks (2015) take a sociocultural approach to second language acquisition and describe the process as one that leads to *multi-competence* or *plurilingualism*, rather than becoming error-free or *native-like* in a target language. Recognizing that learners develop linguistic repertoires in multiple languages, Valdés and her colleagues challenge more traditional views that would describe the process of second language acquisition as a linear progression to acquire a grammatical system and communicative competence in a new language. They also warn against articulating the goal of second language acquisition as becoming *balanced bilinguals*. They argue that a sociocultural perspective has the "potential of informing and enriching the design of classroom environments in which students would be able to experience multiple ways of using both their home language and English for a variety of academic purposes in both their written and oral forms" (70). Based on this philosophy, students at the Bridging level will also be expected to use their rich repertoire of skills in multiple languages.

In addition, students at the Bridging level are well characterized by what Hattie and Yates (2014) refer to as engaging in a deliberate learning process, which is slow in pace and does not often occur without sufficient time, focus, support, monitoring, and practice: "Impressions of quick learning are deceptive for many reasons. Unless the material is strongly meaningful, relevant and timely, it is subject to rapid and substantial forgetting" (113). English learners (ELs) at the Bridging level benefit from multiple meaningful language and literacy experiences that challenge them as well as from sustained opportunities to interact with the new material in English along with peer and teacher support. See Figure 5.2 for how Marisa DeSerio and Tracy Martin create a challenging opportunity for sixth-grade students to engage not only in acquiring and synthesizing new knowledge and skills but also in taking sides and debating their points.

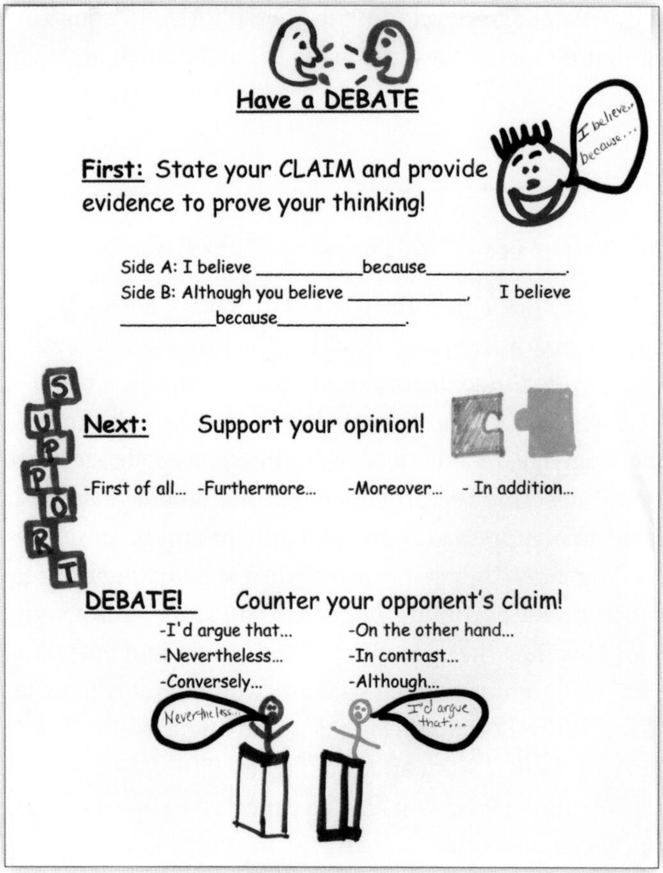

Figure 5.2
Debate Anchor Chart

What Can *Bridging* Level English Learners Do?

ELs who have reached the Bridging level of language proficiency continue to represent a range of language and literacy skills across the four domains. Language acquisition is still fluid, individual, and ever changing, so continue to expect your ELs to demonstrate different levels of skills in listening, speaking, reading, or writing. In this chapter, we will continue the previously established asset-based exploration of what ELs can do and how their teachers can further support their growth. We must recognize that language acquisition is a dynamic process that does not end when a child achieves the highest level of language proficiency. As before, we cannot allow a label to define a child and must look at each student as an individual learner.

A shared unique characteristic of Bridging level students is their demonstrated success of acquiring advanced skills across all four domains: they can read and comprehend complex texts; they can express themselves orally and in writing across topics, both familiar and unfamiliar to them; and they maintain both personal and academic dialogues with increasing confidence. They can also take on leadership roles and support ELs at lower levels of proficiency as their role models and bilingual peer bridges. See Figure 5.3 for two of Rupali Nagpal's first-grade students (supported by English language development specialist Anjali Sengupta) on two different language proficiency levels. Notice how the developing student looks to his peer for support and affirmation.

When it comes to *listening*, you can expect evidence of high levels of English comprehension. Bridging level students are likely to be able to:

Figure 5.3 Bridging Level Student Working with Developing Level Partner

→ understand main ideas, supporting details, speaker's purpose, and other more nuanced aspects of oral language

→ make most inferences based on what is presented orally

→ understand multistep directions

→ understand and respond to both everyday and academic conversations of increasing length and complexity

→ process digital recordings (both audio and video) with confidence

→ comprehend increasingly demanding, contextualized, and decontextualized oral presentations

→ attempt to make sense of unfamiliar colloquial expressions, cultural references, and idioms or proverbs.

Regarding *speaking* skills, you will notice that ELs at the Bridging level will:

→ participate in formal and informal conversations with confidence and clarity

→ speak fluently about familiar and academic topics in small- or large-group settings

→ maintain extended dialogues with peers and teachers

→ communicate fluently and spontaneously with minimal hesitation, self-correction, or rephrasing

→ use a comprehensive repertoire of sentence structures and complex grammatical structures

→ make phonological, syntactic, or semantic errors that don't impede the overall meaning of the communication

→ confidently offer prepared academic presentations

→ integrate a rich variety of grade- and age-appropriate words, including technical or colloquial expressions, yet may encounter challenges with figurative language such as metaphors, idioms, or proverbs as well as less commonly known idiomatic expressions.

When it comes to *reading,* your Bridging level students will demonstrate more complex skills as they begin to:

→ read and understand texts on familiar as well as novel topics with appropriate speed and fluency

→ read for enjoyment and academic purposes with fluency

→ comprehended all main ideas and supporting details in increasingly more complex academic texts

→ develop new learning by reading texts on unfamiliar topics

→ figure out meanings of new words and complex sentences using context clues and prior knowledge or other linguistic resources

> → make sense of complex texts using various comprehension strategies, occasionally requiring scaffolds and supports

> → continue to find idiomatic expressions and words with multiple meanings challenging.

See Figure 5.4 for Yara Graupera's effort to help her middle school students recognize Greek and Latin roots in academic vocabulary.

With *writing,* Bridging level students will be able to:

> → effectively communicate ideas related to familiar and academic topics

> → write for personal and academic purposes with increasing fluency and length

> → demonstrate control over increasingly more complex grammatical structures, but may make errors in syntax and word choice

> → take notes based on information they read or listen to with increasing accuracy and detail

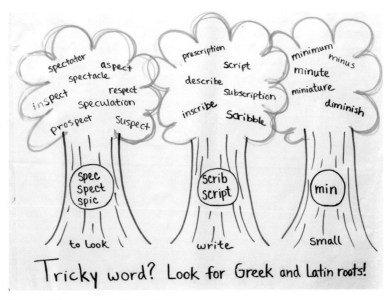

Figure 5.4 Latin and Greek Roots

→ write in all major grade-appropriate academic genres (narrative, expository, persuasive) although may continue to encounter challenges with discipline-specific vocabulary or complex sentence structures

→ organize ideas into logical, well-developed text with errors in word choice or grammar that do not interfere with meaning

→ produce written texts of various length and purpose with minimal errors that do not impede the overall meaning.

In Figure 5.5 see an excerpt from a Bridging level student's essay about earthquakes. Notice how her teacher, Kathy Lameras, asked the student to add marginal annotations to help make her writing more organized and focused.

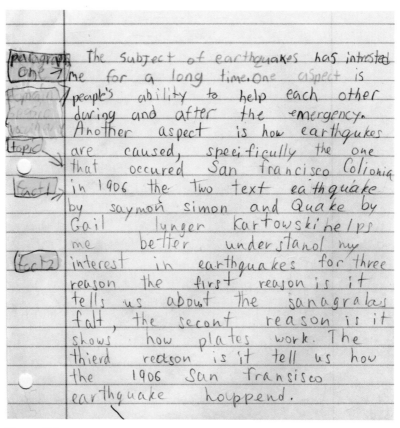

Figure 5.5   Marginal annotations help students stay organized.

In general, students at the Bridging level demonstrate increased independence and fluency in all four language skills as well as with academic literacy skills. This growth supports their language and literacy development across a variety of grade- and age-appropriate academic settings. Remember Jetta and Francis from the beginning of the chapter? Although both are identified as Bridging level students, their areas of strengths and needs for further growth differ significantly. Jetta enjoys writing and produces longer, more elaborate pieces with success. She recently began to facilitate some of the student-led discussions her teachers designed for her class. Although students talking to each other and maintaining academic conversations on their own are challenging skills, her teachers recognize the need to nurture her independence and leadership skills. They also know that whether students are highly proficient ELs or English speakers, question starters and modeling can continue to help prepare for and guide these discussions. Francis, on the other hand, is a confident conversationalist and fluent interpreter using three languages. He thrives in an environment where he can talk, explain his thoughts, and use his advanced facility with multiple languages. His writing skills need more attention so his teachers continue to help him organize his ideas into logical, well-developed written pieces.

What Practices Support *Bridging* Level Students?

Although the broad-brush descriptions here will help understand what your ELs can do, Bridging level students need continued opportunities to build academic language skills in all four domains. Students at the Bridging level will be best supported through teaching techniques that appropriately challenge them linguistically and academically. See Figure 5.6 for an excerpt from Jennifer Delahunt's reading conference notes that reveal differentiated support and highly individualized feedback to her fifth-grade students based on their proficiency levels.

Bridging level students need learning activities that encourage them to take further risks with the language and use their full linguistic repertoires in English and their home languages (rather than replacing and substituting their first language entirely).

With these students, continue to enhance their comprehension of increasingly complex language and context and involve them in more precise and more extended language production. Some practices designed to challenge Bridging

	Reading Conference Notes on Emerging, Expanding, and Bridging Level Students		
Name (Proficiency level)	**Strategy Taught**	**Notes**	**Next Steps Offered**
Kayla (Emerging level)	Authors use adjectives to describe feelings.	Kayla and I noticed how authors use adjectives to describe feelings. We acted out the words using facial expressions and body movements.	"In the next chapter, mark two places when the author uses adjectives to describe the character's feelings."
Ali (Developing level)	Judgment words (such as *bad, good, best, brave, worst, most, beautiful,* and *dangerous*) and actions give us information about characters.	Ali and I looked for judgment words and corresponding actions to learn more about each character.	"Continue to spot places in the book when the author gives us information about characters through the use of judgment words and character actions."
Hector (Bridging level)	End-of-sentence punctuation marks give the reader clues about the purpose of each sentence.	Hector and I read pages in the chapter together and changed our voice based on punctuation. We talked about the purpose of each punctuation mark.	"As you read, continue to notice end-of-sentence punctuation and mark places where you think the punctuation mark was used for a different purpose."

Figure 5.6   Developed by Jennifer Walters Delahunt

level ELs in all four language domains at the highest possible levels are to: (1) listen to and discuss podcasts and other digital recordings, (2) encourage reading logs, and (3) start a language study book.

Listen to and Discuss Podcasts and Digital Audio Recordings

Listening to rapid speech without visual support may present a special challenge for all ELs, even those at the highest language proficiency levels. When an oral presentation or even a teacher read-aloud is lengthy or happens to be on an unfamiliar topic, Bridging level ELs may lose focus, get stuck on some unfamiliar detail, or otherwise struggle with making a necessary inference or connection. To build up stamina, begin with multimedia presentations that students at the Bridging level may *view* and *listen to* at the same time. For more information, see the strategies section later in this chapter.

Podcasts or digitally recorded books present a unique opportunity for students to make sense of material that is delivered with limited or no visuals (Parris, Estrada, and Honigsfeld 2017). Listening builds stamina and making meaning based on oral input. Rather than isolate ELs and place them in the back of the room with a headset, remember to make this a collaborative, socially engaging activity that requires students not only to listen but to discuss and deconstruct meaning as well. Continued opportunities for oral expression including teacherless conversations (Breslin and Ambrose 2013) are important. ELs at similar language proficiency or English speakers may all be part of a listening station activity that includes guided note-taking tasks and discussions, such as the template in Figure 5.7. Figure 5.8 shows how engaged Bethel Aster and Katie Toppel's student is when listening to a digital recording.

Encourage Reading Logs

When ELs at advanced proficiency levels have difficulty understanding complex texts, it is frequently caused by a lack of familiarity with the topic, people, events, or perspectives presented in the text. I will always remember a second-grade class I once cotaught. There was a story in the literacy program about the *Titanic*. Despite the vivid descriptions in the text, the prereading strategies we applied, and the visuals, one student raised her hand and asked, "What is the *Titanic*?" Somehow, she missed that it was an ocean liner. It was a humbling moment. The same can be true of a child first learning about the Erie Canal, Westward expansion, or Rosa Parks, even if they demonstrate higher levels of language proficiency. Students at the Bridging level will benefit from using a tool like a reading log to keep track of their understanding of texts.

A reading log is also known as a reading diary, reading journal, or response journal. It is designed to help students document what they understood in the text. You can either encourage students to write down some required information (you can assign certain focal points) or, better yet, invite students to select their own ways of keeping track of their reading and documenting their new

Listening Station Directions
and Guided Note-Taking Template

As you listen to the story about _____, complete the following steps:

First Listening

1. Start listening to the podcast at the same time as your peers.

2. Listen to the entire podcast without stopping or rewinding.

3. When finished, take your headsets off and share your answers to the following questions. Make sure everyone at your station has a turn.

   a. What was the story about?

   b. What else would you like to find out about _____?

Second Listening

4. Set the timer to _____ minutes. This is how much time you will have to listen to the podcast again and take notes. Listen to the podcast once more, and this time feel free to stop the recording or rewind it as needed to be able to take notes in the following listening grid:

Questions:	My Answers	My Listening Partner's Answers
Question 1		
Question 2		

5. Use Flipgrid (www.flipgrid.com) to record your own ninety-second review of the podcast. Remember to include three main points in your review using our SEA acronym:

   a. **Summary:** What was the podcast about? (What is the main message of the podcast?)

   b. **Evaluation:** What was done well, and what could be improved in this podcast? (What did you like or dislike about it? What did you value or appreciate, or what was missing or lacking?)

   c. **Application:** How does the message of the podcast apply to you?

Figure 5.7   Listening Station Directions and Guided Note-Taking Template

learning. Consider technology and multimodal ways of expressing new learning to motivate your students. See Figure 5.9 for technological tools that may augment or replace traditional reading logs.

Students at the Bridging level will benefit from reading widely (to further expand their background knowledge and to build new frames of reference) and reading deeply (to develop expertise in unique topics of interest and to foster curiosity and motivation for

Figure 5.8 Third grader listens to a story on his iPad.

Technological Tools That May Augment or Replace Traditional Written Response	
Name of Technological Tool	**What the Tool Does**
Notability https://www.gingerlabs.com/	Readers can take notes directly in the app or scan in print pages (such as snapshots of pages from a book they read) and add text markups or annotations digitally
LiveBinders http://www.livebinders.com/	Keeps all reading logs together in one digital place
Tellagami https://tellagami.com/	Allows readers to create an avatar (character) and record responses to readings through digital voice recordings
VoiceThread https://voicethread.com/	Records and shares responses to readings through digital voice recordings
Book Creator https://bookcreator.com/	Combines text, images, video and audio responses to readings
Green Screen https://greenscreen.com/	Creates professional-looking edited videos

Figure 5.9 Technological Tools to Support Writing

more independent reading). Reading for enjoyment and developing lifelong reading and writing habits are just as important as reading for academic purposes. Encourage students to read for enjoyment by making reading materials such as comic books, sports magazine, kids' versions of *National Geographic* or *Time* magazine, and so on. Figure 5.10 shows Jamie Hoesing's second-grade students fully engaged in reading surrounded by their peers.

Start a Language Study Book

Expect Bridging level students to continue to be challenged by language features and conceptual complexity when they read grade-level academic texts, listen to others, or try to express themselves orally and in writing. They might have become very good at guessing some word meanings, figuring out some longer sentences, and getting the gist of all texts (whether presented in a print format or orally). Yet, they are very likely also to encounter words, sentences,

Figure 5.10   A comfy corner invites more engaged reading.

and texts that are not fully comprehensible, thus remain confusing or disconnected for them.

TESOL (2018) identified the characteristics of proficient academic English at the word, sentence, discourse, and conceptual levels. The rich and highly specialized vocabulary, the syntactic complexity of long sentences, and the density of texts presented across a variety of topics and genres may present challenges to the most proficient ELs. In addition, conceptual level characteristics to pay attention to include:

> → developing language skills for a range of cognitive functions (such as describing, analyzing, and evaluating)

> → offering adequate details in writing and speech

> → understanding and communicating about abstract concepts

> → maintaining objectivity by separating the speaker from the subject and employing logical reasoning.

One way to ensure that students seek deeper understanding and seek support from you as needed is to invite them to keep a language study book. In Chapter 1, I introduced personal dictionaries that may serve more advanced learners as well. In a personal dictionary, students organize self-selected words alphabetically and may add a student-friendly definition of their own. On the other hand, a language study book is organized by content or by using a thematic approach, and it can be dedicated to just the science or social studies topics covered.

Digital tools may also be used for language work and replace the traditional paper-and-pencil versions of personal dictionaries and language study books. Create a Google form that students can use to collect language chunks such as idiomatic expressions, phrases, and unique vocabulary and then engage in dialogue with each other and you when these forms are shared. Tonya Schepers (in collaboration with Aaron Wiles) has her eighth graders develop ownership of complex words by contributing digital notebook pages to a shared Google folder. Figure 5.11 shows Tonya's example, which the students used as a model for their own work. See how one student defined *revert* in Figure 5.12.

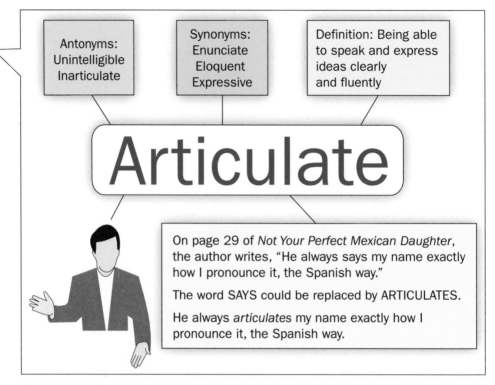

Figure 5.11 Teacher Model of Complex Vocabulary Cards

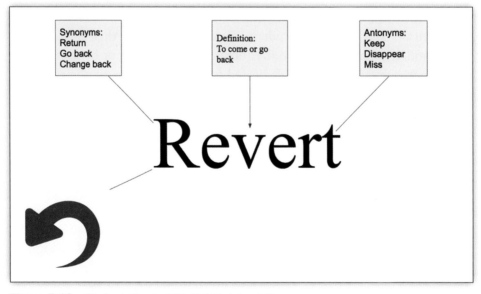

Figure 5.12 Student-Created Digital Notebook Page

What Strategies Will Help *Bridging* Level Students Most?

Visual Support

Throughout the book I have suggested using digital media to build receptive language skills. When students listen to authentic language through audio recordings, the digital media offers many advantages: they can stop, pause, and repeat anything they want to hear more than once, and depending on the device in use, they can even control the rate of speech. Similarly, when students have access to video recordings, they can take advantage of the built-in features, using subtitles, pausing, stopping, rewinding, or watching multiple times. Instructional videos and resources may be subscription based (check with your school librarian) or available free of charge. Figures 5.13 and 5.14 show how Nikole Emerson and Katie Toppel's kindergarteners and Mary Langon's sixth graders regularly consult electronic sources for independent reading, for partner work, to record their spoken language to scaffold their writing, or to clarify the meaning of words, sentences, and texts.

Figure 5.13 Kindergarteners get savvy and use technology with ease.

Figure 5.14 Students use technological tools and each other as they work in pairs to do research.

As you plan learning experiences for ELs that include digital tools, consider the essential dimensions of digital and media literacy—in addition to and in alignment with language development—as outlined by Hobbs (2011). As you decide on tools and tasks, reflect with your colleagues using the following questions after each of Hobbs' digital literacy dimensions.

→ **Access:** Do students have an opportunity to find and share appropriate and relevant information and use media texts and technological tools effectively?

→ **Analyze:** Do students use critical thinking to analyze digital content including message purpose, target audience, quality, credibility, point of view, and potential effects or consequences of messages?

→ **Create:** Do students compose or generate content using creativity and confidence in self-expression, with awareness of purpose, audience, and composition techniques?

→ **Reflect:** Do students consider the impact of media messages and technological tools upon their own thinking and their actions in daily life?

→ **Act:** Do students work individually and collaboratively to share knowledge and solve problems in school and in their community?

As always, digital tools are just that—*tools*—to augment and not replace the teaching-learning process that happens through ongoing, authentic interactions among students and between students and their teachers. Traditional visual support remains just as important. See Figure 5.15 for Laura Fuentes' diagram about the Crusades to help her seventh graders fully grasp the lesson.

Learning by Doing

Digital storytelling and multimedia projects inspired by maker education may lead to new and exciting opportunities for student self-expression. These technology-enhanced learning approaches allow students at all proficiency levels to express themselves in multimodal and multilingual ways. Regardless of age, linguistic, or cultural background, an increasing number of students belong to the "iGeneration" (Rosen 2011). What sets them apart from other generations is that

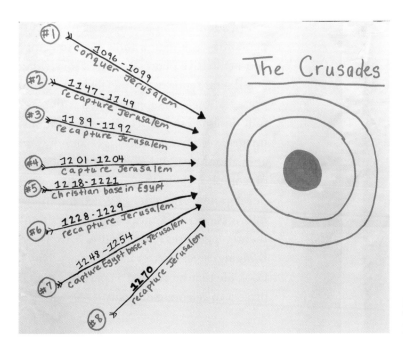

Figure 5.15
The Crusades
Diagram

many of their lives have been shaped by technology, by "being online, using computers offline, listening to music, playing video games, talking on the telephone, instant messaging, texting, sending and receiving e-mail, and watching television" (12). Digital storytelling and multimedia projects tap into this reality.

Digital Storytelling and Reporting

Traditional storytelling and expository writing are powerful ways to have ELs communicate their ideas. When students engage in digital creation, a new dimension is added to these strategies. As a result, students can also exercise digital citizenship as well as practice twenty-first-century literacy skills that require technology integration. Burnett (2015) reminds us that digital storytelling allows for immigrant experiences to be shared and empathy to be developed in others.

> *Telling stories is an innately human experience that connects us with others and creates a sense of belonging. Hearing another person's perspective is also a key component of empathy. Finally, writing family immigration stories—no matter how distant or recent—helps students read, reflect upon, and empathize with the common threads and variations of American narratives (part 2).*

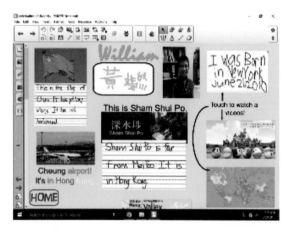

Figure 5.16   Smart Notebook Page

In addition to personal narratives, students may use digital tools for expository and persuasive genres as well. Storytelling and digital reporting come alive when oral presentations are supplemented with carefully designed slides rich with photographs, images, voiceover recordings, sounds, and animation. In addition, students make use of complex skills they already have and develop new ones while SWiRL-ing (more information in the next section) with authentic purposes. See Figure 5.16 for a Bridging level first-grader's Smart Notebook file that he created as part of a digital project to celebrate diversity.

Multimedia Projects

Maker education is built upon constructivist philosophy, and it "views learning as a highly personal endeavor requiring the student, rather than the teacher, to initiate the learning process . . . teachers act as guides for inquiry-based approaches to the development of knowledge and thinking processes" (Kurti, Kurti, and Fleming 2014, 8). In the tradition of maker education, you may use everyday household items or technological tools to encourage students to create a new product. In the process, students will be engaged in all four language skills, or the SWiRL-ing classroom. See Figure 5.17 for a specially designated Makerspace/STEAM Lab at Judy Jacobs Parkway Elementary School in the Plainview-Old Bethpage School District, Long Island, New York.

You might have seen the idea of a SWRL-ing or SWiRL-ing classrooms in some other sources. The common notion is the importance of integrating the four language domains and shifting the order from listening, speaking, reading, and writing to speaking, writing, reading, and listening (Honigsfeld and Dodge 2015). Burkins and Yaris (2013) and Cooper (2012) blogged about it, emphasizing the need for active engagement with language and literacy tasks. Anderson (2015) suggests that "language components are interrelated following a format of SWiRL (speaking and writing integrated with reading and listening) that give opportunity for social and academic language development in a holistic and meaningful way" (73). Here, I will interpret the *I* of SWiRL as

Figure 5.17 Makerspaces invite creativity and engaged learning.

students interacting with each other and complex materials. While using the constructivist approach of maker education and creating original tactile and digital products, students will:

Speak to each other to discuss the available resources and plan the project.

Write, sketch, or draw to identify the steps necessary for completing the activity.

Interact with each other as they negotiate the product design and completion.

Read and use print and digital resources that inform their steps in completing the project.

Listen to each other as well as to digitally available video or audio recordings that are relevant to the project.

See Figure 5.18 for Jennifer Gingerich and Maryann Lo Duca-Peik's English language learner/K–3 intervention classroom where third graders work in collaboration to create a response and present their work to their classmates.

Figure 5.18 Third-grade students present work to classmates.

Ferlazzo and Hull-Sypnieski (2018) suggest creating a book review trailer. Invite your students to select their favorite book and video-record a short trailer that introduces the book (without giving away the ending) and offers two or three reasons why they liked the book and why other students should read it.

> *Remember—a trailer is like a commercial—you are trying to "sell" this book to someone. Be convincing and support your opinions with specific reasons. You will need to show the book while you are talking about it. Be creative and practice, practice, practice! (14)*

Keep in mind that your students need opportunities to compose in print and nonprint genres. There is a high level of intrinsic motivation associated with learning opportunities that engage creativity, projects, and digital tools for expression. Such projects do not take place in a vacuum; instead, they are embedded in a context in which they can further develop ELs' communication and collaboration skills.

Oral Language Development

Socrates is well known for his use of questions to help his disciples think critically and arrive at their own answers. Similarly, if you try Socratic circles or Socratic seminars, your students learn to take ownership of the classroom discourse by contributing both questions and answers. During Socratic circles students are typically divided into two groups, the inner and the outer circle, with each assuming different roles, and the teacher acts as the facilitator for the activity as a target text is explored (Staehr Fenner and Snyder 2014). The inside circle is designated to be the discussion group, and the outside circle observes the discussion and takes notes. Simple, yet clear rules of participation need to be established, See Figure 5.19 for a set of rules I created for fourth- and fifth-grade students.

The Socratic circle helps ELs at the Bridging level to further develop their listening, verbal, and critical thinking skills. Furthermore, students will continue to benefit from anchor charts with precise academic language and sentence frames displayed in the room so that students can refer to them during a discussion (Soto 2014). To not only participate but lead classroom discourse offers students opportunities to use their "knowledge about language to use language" (Rex et al. 2010, 95). In addition, ELs assert themselves as leaders in the classroom and shift their position from one that requires assistance and support to one that clearly indicates potential. Keep in mind, though: you do not have to wait until students reach the Bridging level to help them claim their place in the classroom as students of potential, promise, and success!

Reading Support

There can be a significant difference when students read in a science class versus social studies or math. Shanahan and Shanahan (2008) were among the first to define literacy instruction by distinguishing among three levels of literacy. In their framework,

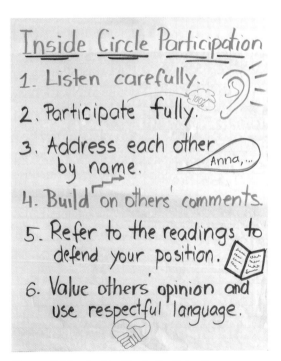

Figure 5.19 Inside Circle Participation

level 1, or *basic literacy*, refers to understanding letter-sound correspondence, decoding, and accessing high-frequency words that are necessary for all reading tasks. Level 2, or *intermediate literacy*, designates skills that are common to many reading tasks such as developing basic fluency when reading, understanding generic academic words and phrases, and applying general comprehension strategies to everyday and academic readings. Level 3, or *disciplinary literacy*, specifies literacy skills that are essential to understanding and producing text that is unique to the various content areas, such as literature, history, science, mathematics, music, or any other subject matter.

Students at the Bridging level of language proficiency have mastered all the foundational reading skills as well as comprehension skills that allow them to meet the typical requirements of grade-level literacy tasks. However, to successfully navigate rigorous core content readings, ELs need opportunities to engage in higher-level literacy tasks that challenge them to integrate multiple literacy roles (Fang 2012).

1. As *code breakers*, ELs access a range of skills and resources to process print and nonprint input (signs, symbols, visual, and graphic representations of information).

2. As *meaning makers*, ELs interact with the target text and with each other to understand the overall message, to unpack the layers of meaning in the text, and to discover the more subtle implications of the readings.

3. As *text users*, ELs have regular and meaningful access to a range of texts written in different genres for different audiences and purposes. These target texts also serve an authentic purpose in the students' academic and literacy development to ensure high levels of motivation and engagement.

4. As *text analysts and critics*, ELs critically interpret, analyze, synthesize, and evaluate multiple texts.

The ultimate goal is to engage students in SWiRL-ing and thinking across all content areas in discipline-specific ways. Two key strategies for ELs to practice these literacy roles with a special focus on disciplinary literacy are text multiplication and inquiry-based learning.

Text Multiplication

Text pairing has been well established. It supports the idea that students should explore a topic by reading at least two different selections related to each other. One popular way to pair texts is to invite students to read a fiction and a nonfiction piece on the same topic, thus developing a deeper appreciation for the text features of each type of texts. To challenge and further expand the literacy skills of students at the Bridging level, develop a system for not just pairing but multiplying texts. In addition to your basic paired texts, locate several additional authentic, real-life reading selections. They can come from websites, news articles (or headlines), blogs, advertisements, food labels, song lyrics, manuals, charts, and diagrams. See Figure 5.20 for a summary of Web-based resources offering safe content.

While students engage with multiple texts, they develop an appreciation for the diversity of genres and text types available to readers, and they learn to detect ways in which language is used differently depending on the source. Reading across genres and text types will help them make connections among texts and topics.

Bridging ELs may work independently or collaboratively to engage in critical reading and note-taking across multiple texts. I-charts, or inquiry charts,

---

Scholastic News (https://scholasticnews.scholastic.com/)

Time for Kids (http://www.timeforkids.com/)

Big Backyard or *Ranger Rick* (https://blog.nwf.org/2011/09/big-backyard-new-name-same-amazing-magazine/ *and* www.rangerrick.org/RangerRick)

National Geographic Kids (http://kids.nationalgeographic.com/kids)

Audiobooks for Children (http://storynory.com)

Think TV via PBS Learning Media (https://thinktv.pbslearningmedia.org)

A makerspace for the Humanities (https://www.awesomestories.com)

Watch Know Learn (http://www.watchknowlearn.org/default.aspx) (preK–12 videos organized by theme)

Kids Know It Network (https://kidsknowit.com/videos/) (K–8 science, math, social studies videos and additional visual resources)

Figure 5.20   Websites and Magazines That Provide Student-Friendly, Safe Content

were originally developed by Hoffman in 1992; yet, they continue to serve as an effective tool for analysis. The adapted template in Figure 5.21 offers a structured framework for your students to explore multiple sources to answer the same guiding questions. Alternately, you can try collaborative or jigsaw reading/writing in which each group focuses on one source only and completes one column of the chart.

Inquiry-Based Learning

When students engage in meaningful, deep explorations focused on content area topics, their learning will be more substantial. Inquiry-based learning recognizes that students' curiosity and desire to understand drive learning, in other words: "One remarkable characteristics of inquiry is that it is done *by* the individual not *to* the individual, and this active form of learning . . . is what makes knowledge stick" (Lent 2016, 104). In Figure 5.22 students plan an inquiry-based science research project in Katherine Lameras' fifth-grade classroom.

Although inquiry-based learning may be implemented by individual students, when done collaboratively, students benefit from shared learning op-

I-Chart Template				
Topic	Source 1	Source 2	Source 3	Source 4
Title and Author				
Text Type				
Question 1				
Question 2				
Question 3				
Summary				

Figure 5.21

portunities and interactions with each other and the material. Banchi and Bell (2008) suggest that there are four levels of inquiry, with incrementally more complex expectations for student independence. Figure 5.23 shows the four levels, their purpose, and a brief summary of what students and teachers do.

Based on the age, grade, and level of complexity of the content you teach, select the type of inquiry that is most appropriate—challenging but not frustrating—thus best supporting your students' natural curiosity. Figure 5.24 is an anchor chart that reviews the steps of the inquiry process with fourth-grade students.

Figure 5.22 Reviewing Text-Based Evidence and Planning a Joint Research Project

Banchi and Bell's Levels of Inquiry				
Inquiry Type	**Purpose**	**What Students Do**	**What Teachers Provide**	**Examples from the Classroom**
Confirmation inquiry	To introduce the inquiry process	Confirm through experience what they already know	Questions Procedure Solution	Hot air pops popcorn.
Structured inquiry	To scaffold the inquiry process	Generate an explanation for what they find	Questions Procedure	Watering plants with vinegar vs. water will result in "acid-rain-like" conditions and will cause the plants to die.
Guided inquiry	To provide a more open-ended process for students	Design the procedure of inquiry, and generate explanations	Questions	What do magnets attract?
Open inquiry	To give students ownership of the inquiry process	Design the question and the method of inquiry as well as generate explanations	Process reminders and expectations	How can we start a recycling program in our school? What is climate change, and how can I explain the science to my peers? What is the science behind sword making?

Figure 5.23

Adapted from Banchi and Bell (2008)

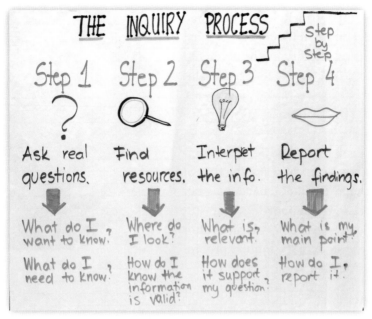

Figure 5.24
Inquiry Process
Anchor Chart

Writing Support

Similar to reading, the expectations for what types of writing students need to do will vary based on the content area. Calkins, Ehrenworth, and Lehman (2012) suggest that:

> (O)nce students become fluent, fast, structured, and proficient writers across a range of genres, it is easy to take those skills on the road, using writing as a tool for thinking across all the disciplines. When students write across the curriculum, it not only escalates their engagement in other subjects but also makes teachers more accountable and more responsive. (p. 14)

They need "time for practice, time to share writing, time to complete pieces of writing, and time to respond to and evaluate all of that writing" (Kirby and Crowitz 2012, 9). They also need to see writing as a tool for thinking, and they need opportunities to further develop their ability to do so. See Figure 5.25 for Lisa Wittek's anchor chart that shows students how to dig deeper and offer more details in their writing and Figure 5.26 for one of Nicole Fernandez's Bridging level first-grade student's independent writing.

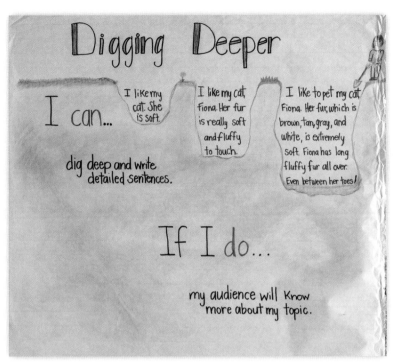

Figure 5.25
Writing More Complex Sentences with a Visual Anchor Chart as a Reminder

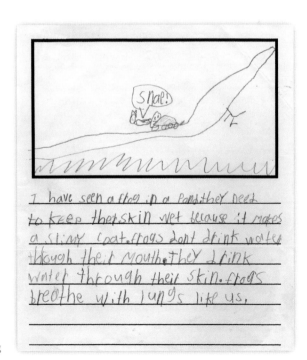

Figure 5.26
A First-Grade Bridging Level Student's Writing

Offer Feedback

For writing to improve, ELs need to share and receive feedback on their writing. The feedback should encourage them to reflect on their own writing and encourage revisions to word choice, sentence structure, paragraph organization, and meaning (Anderson 2018). There are multiples ways to offer feedback to student writing.

→ Conduct regular writing conferences. Sit with students one-on-one and get to know them as writers. Try to articulate students' strengths and teach specific strategies that will help improve their writing.

→ Offer written feedback. Students sometimes want to take time to read and reflect on your feedback. Ask students if they would prefer comments directly in their notebook/paper or on sticky notes.

→ Teach students to offer each other feedback. You can scaffold their partner work with some sentence stems posted on an anchor chart or printed on a piece of paper:

- When I read this part, I wanted to know more about _____.

- What would you want your readers to know more about _____?

- I noticed _____, and I wondered _____.

- Could you include more details on _____?

- Could you make connections to _____ here?

- When I read this part, I had a question about _____?

When Are *Bridging* Level Students Ready to Move On?

Although most schools determine levels of language proficiency and student placement based on annual standardized assessments such as ACCESS by WIDA, ELPA21, and NYSESLAT, formative assessments and progress monitoring play an important role in your day-to-day work with ELs. To track the progress *Bridging* level students make, continue with a multidimensional approach. Your data collection should include teacher observations of oral language skills (listening and speaking), student work samples to document how their writing skills develop, and reading conferences where you can check on their comprehension and also monitor how their reading skills grow and to what degree they are able to use reading strategies.

You will start to notice that Bridging level students are developing full capacity with the grade-level target language skills level when you can remove even more scaffolds, or when their participation in all types of language and literacy learning activities approximates that of proficient English-speaking peers. For example, comparable to her English-speaking peers, Jetta is likely to be able to read grade- and age-appropriate texts with minimal support. And Francis will make even fewer syntactic or semantic errors in his writing, which will also improve in length and complexity. Both students will recognize and begin to use figurative and idiomatic expressions that are not as common.

References

Afflerbach, P., B. Y. Cho, J.Y. Kim, M. E. Crasses, and B. Doyle. 2013. "Reading: What Else Matters Besides Skills?" *The Reading Teacher* 66: 440–48.

Agirdag, O. 2009. "All Languages Welcomed Here." *Educational Leadership* 66 (7): 20–25.

Aguilar, E. 2016. *The Art of Coaching Teams: Building Resilient Communities That Transform Schools.* San Francisco: Jossey-Bass.

Anderson, C. 2018. *A Teacher's Guide to Writing Conferences: Classroom Essentials.* Portsmouth, NH: Heinemann.

Anderson, E. F. 2015. "Engaging and Effective Strategies for English Language Learners." In *Accelerating and Extending Literacy for Diverse Students*, edited by D. Sisk, 66–83. Latham, MD: Rowman and Littlefield.

Anderson, J. 2005. *Mechanically Inclined: Building Grammar, Usage, and Style into Writer's Workshop.* Portland, ME: Stenhouse.

———. 2017. "No More Think, Pair, Share!" http://www.grnewsletters.com/archive /habitsofmind/No-More-Think-Pair-Share-474383203.html?e=&u=9Uv6&s =y4sjPh.

Applebee, A. N., J. A. Langer, M. Nystrand, and A. Gamoran. 2003. "Student Performance in Middle and High School English Discussion-Based Approaches to Developing Understanding: Classroom Instruction and Student Performance in Middle and High School English." *American Educational Research Journal* 40: 685–730. doi:10.3102/00028312040003685.

Asher, J. J. 1981. "The Total Physical Response: Theory and Practice." *Annals of the New York Academy of Sciences* 379: 324–31.

Ayer, L. 2018. "4 Things All Project-Based Learning Teachers Should Do." https:// www.teachthought.com/project-based-learning/4-things-project-based -learning-teachers/.

Baker, S., N. Lesaux, M. Jayanthi, J. Dimino, C. P. Proctor, J. Morris, R. Gersten, K. Haymond, M. J. Kieffer, S. Linan-Thompson, and R. Newman-Gonchar. 2014. *Teaching Academic Content and Literacy to English Learners in Elementary and Middle School* (NCEE 2014-4012). Washington, DC: National Center for Education Evaluation and Regional Assistance (NCEE), Institute of Education Sciences, U.S. Department of Education. http://ies.ed.gov/ncee/wwc/publications _reviews.aspx.

Bambrick-Santoyo, P. A., A. Settles, and J. Worrell. 2013. *Great Habits, Great Readers: A Practical Guide to K–4 Reading in Light of the Common Core.* San Francisco: Jossey-Bass.

Banchi, H., and R. Bell. 2008. "The Many Levels of Inquiry." *Science and Children* 46 (2): 26–29.

Barber, D., and D. Foord. 2014. "From English Teacher to Learner Coach." www.the -round.com.

Beck, I. L., M. G. McKeown, and L. Kucan. 2013. *Bringing Words to Life: Robust Vocabulary Instruction*, Second edition. New York: Guilford.

Billings, E., and A. Walqui. n.d. "De-Mystifying Complex Texts: What Are 'Complex' Texts and How Can We Ensure ELLs/MLLs Can Access Them?" http://www .nysed.gov/common/nysed/files/programs/bilingual-ed/de-mystifying_complex _texts-2.pdf.

Blachowicz, C., P. Fisher, D. Ogle, and S. Watts-Taffe. 2013. *Teaching Academic Vocabulary K–8: Effective Practices Across the Curriculum.* New York: Guilford.

Bligh, C. 2014. *The Silent Experiences of Young Bilingual Learners: A Sociocultural Study into the Silent Period.* Rotterdam, The Netherlands: Sense.

Boyd, M. P., and L. Galda. 2011. *Real Talk in Elementary Classrooms: Effective Oral Language Practice.* New York: Guilford Press.

Breslin, P. M., and Ambrose, R. 2013. Teacherless Discussion: Engaging Middle School Students Through Peer-to-Peer Talk. In *Breaking the Mold of Education: Innovative and Successful Practices for Student Engagement, Empowerment, and Motivation,* edited by A. Cohan and A. Honigsfeld. (49–55). Lanham, MD: Rowman and Littlefield.

Bunch, G. C., A. Kibler, and S. Pimentel. 2013. "Realizing Opportunities for English Learners in the Common Core English Language Arts and Disciplinary Literacy Standards." http://ell.stanford.edu/sites/default/files/pdf/academic-papers/01 _Bunch_Kibler_Pimentel_RealizingOpp%20in%20ELA_FINAL_0.pdf.

———. 2014. "Realizing Opportunities for English Learners in the Common Core English Language Arts and Disciplinary Literacy Standards." In *Handbook to Implement Educational Programs, Practices, and Policies for English Learners*, edited by L. Minaya-Rowe. Charlotte, NC: Information Age Publishing.

Burkins, J., and K. Yaris. 2013. "Top Ten Themes of IRA Convention 2013." April 23. www.burkinsandyaris.com/top-ten-themes-of-ira-convention-2013.

Burnett, S. 2015. "Teach Empathy with Digital Immigration Stories." May 28. https://www.edutopia.org/blog/teach-empathy-digital-immigration-stories-sara-burnett.

Calhoun, E. F. 1999. *Teaching Beginning Reading and Writing with the Picture Word Inductive Model.* Alexandria, VA: ASCD.

Calkins, L., M. Ehrenworth, and C. Lehman. 2012. *Pathways to the Common Core: Accelerating Achievement.* Portsmouth, NH: Heinemann.

Canagarajah, A. S. 2013. *Literacy as Translingual Practice: Between Communities and Classrooms.* New York: Routledge.

Cappello, M., and Walker, N. T. 2016. "Visual Thinking Strategies: Teachers' Reflections on Closely Reading Complex Visual Texts Within the Disciplines." *The Reading Teacher* 70 (3): 317–325. doi:10.1002/trtr.1523.

Chappuis, J. 2012. "How Am I Doing?" *Feedback for Learning* 70 (1): 36–41.

Christensen, L. 2010. "Putting Out the Linguistic Welcome Mat." *Wisconsin English Journal* 52 (1): 33–37.

Colorín Colorado. n.d. "Welcome Kit for New ELLs." http://www.colorincolorado.org/article/welcome-kit-new-ells.

Cook, H. G., T. Boals, C. Wilmes, and M. Santos. 2008. "Issues in the Development of Annual Measurable Achievement Objectives for WIDA Consortium States" (WCER Working Paper No. 2008-2). https://wcer.wisc.edu/docs/working-papers/Working_Paper_No_2008_02.pdf.

Cooper, A. 2012. "10 Tips for Teaching English-Language Learners: Tools and Techniques for Better Instruction." https://www.edutopia.org/blog/teaching-english-language-learners-ayanna-cooper.

Cummins, J. 2001. *Negotiating Identities: Education for Empowerment for a Diverse Society.* Los Angeles: California Association for Bilingual Education.

———. 2005. "A Proposal for Action: Strategies for Recognizing Heritage Language Competence as a Learning Resource Within the Mainstream Classroom." *Modern Language Journal* 89: 585–92.

Cummins, S. 2017. "The Case for Multiple Texts." *Educational Leadership* 74 (5): 66–71.

Cunningham, P. M., and R. L. Allington. 2011. *Classrooms That Work: They Can All Read and Write.* Boston: Pearson.

de los Ríos, C. V., and K. Seltzer. 2017. "Translanguaging, Coloniality and English Classrooms: An Exploration of Two Bicoastal Urban Classrooms." *Research in the Teaching of English* 52 (1): 55–76.

Discovery Education. 2018. "Discovery Education Virtual Field Trips." http://www
.discoveryeducation.com/Events/virtual-field-trips/explore/.

Dodge, J., and A. Honigsfeld. 2014. *Core Instructional Routines: Go-to Structures for
Effective Literacy Teaching, K–5.* Portsmouth, NH: Heinemann.

Dorfman, L. R., and R. Cappelli. 2007. *Mentor Texts: Teaching Writing Through Children's Literature, K–6.* Portland, ME: Stenhouse.

Dove, M. G., and A. Honigsfeld. 2013. *Common Core for the Not-So-Common Learner,
Grades K–5: English Language Arts Strategies.* Thousand Oaks, CA: Corwin
Press.

Dutro, S., and K. Kinsella. 2010. "English Language Development: Issues and Imple-
mentation at Grades Six Through Twelve." In *Improving Education for English
Learners: Research-Based Approaches*, 151–207. Sacramento, CA: California
Department of Education.

ELPA 2016. "2016 ELPA21 Proficiency Descriptors." https://www.oregon.gov/ode
/educator-resources/assessment/Documents/elpa21_proficiency_descriptors
.pdf.

Esteban-Guitart, M., and L. C. Moll. 2014. "Lived Experience, Funds of Identity and
Education." *Culture & Psychology* 20: 70–81. doi:10.1177/1354067X13515940.

Fairbairn, S. B., and S. Jones-Vo. 2010. *Differentiating Instruction and Assessment
for English Language Learners: A Guide for K–12 Teachers.* Philadelphia, PA:
Caslon.

Fang, Z. 2012. "Approaches to Developing Content Area Literacies: A Synthesis and
a Critique." *Journal of Adolescent & Adult Literacy* 56: 103–107. doi:10.1002
/JAAL.00110.

Ferlazzo, L., and K. Hull-Sypnieski. 2016. Navigating the Common Core with English
Language Learners: Practical Strategies to Develop Higher-Order Thinking
Skills. San Francisco: Jossey-Bass.

———. 2018. *The ELL Teacher's Toolbox: Hundreds of Practical Ideas to Support Your
Students.* San Francisco: Jossey-Bass.

Ferriter, B. 2016. "Turn Feedback into Detective Work." http://blog.williamferriter.com
/2016/02/20/new-slide-turn-feedback-into-detective-work.

Fisher, D., and N. Frey. 2008. *Wordwise and Content Rich: Five Essential Steps to
Teaching Content Vocabulary.* Portsmouth, NH: Heinemann.

———. 2014. *Checking for Understanding: Formative Assessment Techniques for Your
Classroom*, Second Edition. Alexandria, VA: ASCD.

———. 2017. "Show & Tell: A Video Column/Reducing the Impact of Mobility." *Educational Leadership* 75 (1): 82–83.

Fisher, D., N. Frey, and J. Hattie. 2016. *Visible Learning for Literacy, Grades K–12: Implementing the Practices That Work Best to Accelerate Student Learning.* Thousand Oaks, CA: Corwin.

Frey, N., and D. Fisher. 2009. *Learning Words Inside and Out, Grades 1–6: Vocabulary Instruction That Boosts Achievement in All Subject Areas.* Portsmouth, NH: Heinemann.

García, O. 2009. *Bilingual Education in the 21st Century: A Global Perspective.* Malden, MA: Wiley-Blackwell.

Gibbons, P. 2006. *Bridging Discourses in the ESL Classroom: Students, Teachers and Researchers.* New York: Bloomsbury.

———. 2015. *Scaffolding Language Scaffolding Learning: Teaching English Language Learners in the Mainstream Classroom.* Portsmouth, NH: Heinemann.

Goldenberg, C. N. 1992. *Instructional Conversations and Their Classroom Application* (Educational Practice Report 2). Santa Cruz, CA: National Center for Research on Diversity and Second Language Learning, University of California.

Goldenberg, C. 2013. "Unlocking the Research on English Learners: What We Know and Don't Yet Know About Effective Instruction." *American Educator* 37 (2): 4–11, 38.

Goodman, Y., and Owocki, G. 2002. *Kidwatching: Documenting Children's Literacy Development.* Portsmouth, NH: Heinemann.

Gottlieb, M. 2016. *Assessing English Language Learners: Bridges to Educational Equity.* Thousand Oaks, CA: Corwin.

Gottlieb M., and M. Castro. 2017. *Language Power: Key Uses for Accessing Content.* Thousand Oaks, CA: Corwin.

Gottlieb, M., and G. Ernst-Slavit. 2014. *Academic Language in Diverse Classrooms: Definitions and Contexts.* Thousand Oaks, CA: Corwin.

Gray, S. 2016. "How to Use the Cooperative Learning 'Carousel' Strategy." May 12. http://shelleygrayteaching.com/carousel/.

Greene, J. P., C. Hitt, A. Kraybill, and C. A. Bogulski. 2015. "Learning from Live Theater: Students Realize Gains in Knowledge, Tolerance, and More." *Education Next* 15 (1): 54–61.

Greene, J. P., B. Kisida, and D. H. Bowen. 2014. "The Value of Field Trips." *Education Next* 14 (1): 78–86.

———. 2016. "Why Do Field Trips Matter?" *EdNext Podcast*, Episode 59. November 2. http://educationnext.org/the-educational-value-of-field-trips/.

Hakuta, K., M. Santos, and Z. Fang. 2013. "Challenges and Opportunities for language Learning in the Context of the CCSS and the NGSS." *Journal of Adolescent & Adult Literacy* 56: 451–54.

Hattie, J. 2012. *Visible Learning for Teachers.* New York: Routledge.

Hattie, J., and H. Timperley. 2007. "The Power of Feedback." *Review of Educational Research* 77 (1): 81–112.

Hattie, J., and G. C. R. Yates. 2014. *Visible Learning and the Science of How We Learn.* New York: Routledge.

Haynes, J., and D. Zacarian. 2010. *Teaching English Language Learners Across the Content Areas.* Alexandria, VA: ASCD.

Helman, L., C. Rogers, A. Frederick, and M. Struck. 2016. *Inclusive Literacy Teaching: Differentiating Approaches in Multilingual Elementary Classrooms.* New York: Teachers College Press.

Heritage, M., R. Linquanti, and A. Walqui. 2015. *English Language Learners and the New Standards: Developing Language, Content Knowledge, and Analytical Practices in the Classroom.* Cambridge, MA: Harvard Education Press.

Hill, J. D., and K. B. Miller. 2014. *Classroom Instruction That Works with English Language Learners.* 2nd ed. Alexandria, VA: ASCD.

Hobbs, R. 2011. *Digital and Media Literacy: Connecting Culture and Classroom.* Thousand Oaks, CA: Corwin.

Hoffman, J. 1992. "Critical Reading/Thinking Across the Curriculum: Using I-Charts to Support Learning." *Language Arts* 69: 121–27.

Honigsfeld, A. 2009. "Say 'Cheese' and More: ELLs, Cameras and Language Development." *New Teacher Advocate* 16 (4): 10–11.

Honigsfeld, A., and J. Dodge. 2015. *Core Instructional Routines: Go-to Structures for Effective Literacy Teaching, 6–12.* Portsmouth, NH: Heinemann.

Honigsfeld, A., and M. G. Dove. 2013. *Common Core for the Not-So-Common Learner, Grades 6–12: English Language Arts Strategies.* Thousand Oaks, CA: Corwin Press.

IRA CCSS Committee. 2012. "Literacy Implementation Guidance for the ELA Common Core State Standards." https://www.literacyworldwide.org/docs/default -source/where-we-stand/ela-common-core-state-standards-guidance.pdf? sfvrsn=b1a4af8e_8.

Johnson, D. W., and R. Johnson. 1999. *Learning Together and Alone: Cooperative, Competitive, and Individualistic Learning*, Fifth edition. Boston: Allyn & Bacon.

———. 2009. "An Educational Psychology Success Story: Social Interdependence Theory and Cooperative Learning." *Educational Researcher* 38: 365–79. doi: 10.3102/0013189X09339057.

Kagan, S., M. Kagan, and L. Kagan. 2016. *59 Kagan Structures: Proven Engagement Strategies.* San Clemente, CA: Kagan Publishing.

Kirby, D. L. and D. Crovitz. 2012. *Inside Out: Strategies for Teaching Writing*, Fourth Edition. Portsmouth, NH: Heinemann.

Krashen, S. 1982. *Principles and Practice in Second Language Acquisition.* Oxford, United Kingdom: Pergamon Press.

Krashen, S. D., and Terrell, T. D. 1983. *The Natural Approach: Language Acquisition in the Classroom.* New York: Pergamon.

Kucan, L. 2012. "What Is Most Important to Know About Vocabulary?" *The Reading Teacher* 65: 360–66.

Kurti, R. S., D. L. Kurti, and L. Fleming. 2014. "The Philosophy of Educational Makerspaces: Part 1 of Making an Educational Makerspace." *Teacher Librarian* 41 (5): 8–11.

Ladson-Billings, G. 2011." But That's Just Good Teaching! The Case for Culturally Relevant Pedagogy." In *Thinking About Schools: A Foundations of Education Reader*, edited by E. B. Hilty, 107–116. Boulder, CO: Westview Press.

Law, B., and Eckes, M. 2010. *The-More-Than-Just-Surviving-Handbook: ELL for Every Classroom Teacher.* Winnipeg, MB, Canada: Portage and Main Press.

Lent, R. C. 2016. *This Is Disciplinary Literacy: Reading, Writing, Thinking and Doing . . . Content Area by Content Area.* Thousand Oaks, CA: Corwin.

Lenters, K. 2016. "Telling 'A Story of Somebody' Through Digital Scrapbooking: A Fourth Grade Multi-Literacies Project Takes an Affective Turn." *Literacy Research and Instruction* 55: 262–83. http://dx.doi.org/10.1080/19388071.2016.1162234.

Lyman, F. 1981. *The Responsive Classroom Discussion: The Inclusion of All Students. Mainstreaming Digest.* College Park, MD: University of Maryland.

Massaro, D. W. 2017. "Reading Aloud to Children: Benefits and Implications for Acquiring Literacy Before Schooling Begins." *The American Journal of Psychology* 130 (1): 63–72.

McGee, P. 2017. *Feedback That Moves Writers Forward: How to Escape Correcting Mode to Transform Student Writing.* Thousand Oaks, CA: Corwin.

McGroarty, M. 1993. "Cooperative Learning and Second Language Acquisition." In *Cooperative Learning: A Response to Linguistic and Cultural Diversity,* edited by D. D. Holt, 19–46. Washington, DC: Delta Systems and Center for Applied Linguistics.

Miller, D. 2013. *Reading with Meaning: Teaching Comprehension in the Primary Grades.* 2nd ed. Portland, ME: Stenhouse.

Minkel, J. 2018. *Being an English-Language Learner Is Hard: Here Are 5 Ways Teachers Can Make It Easier.* February 7. https://www.edweek.org/tm/articles/2018/02/07/being-an-english-language-learner-is-hard-here.html.

Moll, L. C. 1992. "Bilingual Classroom Studies and Community Analysis: Some Recent Trends." *Educational Researcher* 21 (2): 20–24.

National Education Association. 2015. "How Educators Can Advocate for English Language Learners (ELLs): All In!" http://www.colorincolorado.org/sites/default/files/ELL_AdvocacyGuide2015.pdf

Nora, J. 2013. "Language as the Lever for Elementary-Level English Language Learners." http://vue.annenberginstitute.org/sites/default/files/issues/VUE37.pdf.

Ohta, A. 2001. *Second Language Acquisition Processes in the Classroom: Learning Japanese.* Mahwah, NJ: Lawrence Erlbaum Associates.

Oxford, R. 2017. *Teaching and Researching Language Learning Strategies: Self-Regulation in Context,* Second edition. New York: Routledge.

Pacheco, M. B., S. M. Daniel, and L. C. Pray. 2017. "Scaffolding Practice: Supporting Emerging Bilinguals' Academic Language Use in Two Classroom Communities." *Language Arts* 95: 63–76.

Paris, D. 2012. "Culturally Sustaining Pedagogy: A Needed Change in Stance, Terminology, and Practice." *Educational Researcher* 41: 93–97.

Parker, W. C. 2006. "Public Discourses in Schools: Purposes, Problems, Possibilities." *Educational Researcher* 35(8): 11–18. doi:10.3102/0013189X035008011.

Parris, H., L. Estrada, and A. Honigsfeld. 2016. *ELL Frontiers: Using Technology to Enhance Instruction for English Learners.* Thousand Oaks, CA: Corwin.

Pearson Education. 2012. Interactive Science. http://assets.pearsonschool.com/_mgr/current/201546/sci-6-8.pdf.

Reeves, A. G., and D. L. Braun. 2012. "What If Every Day Was American Indian Day?" In *Breaking the Mold of Education for Culturally and Linguistically Diverse Students Innovative and Successful Practices for the 21st Century,* edited by A. Honigsfeld and A. Cohan, 103–10. Lanham, MD: Rowman & Littlefield.

Rex, L., Bunn, M., Davila, B., Dickinson, H., Carpenter-Ford, A., Gerben, C., McBee-Orzulak, M., and Thompson, H. 2010. "A Review of Discourse Analysis in Literacy Research: Equitable Access." *Reading Research Quarterly* 45 (1), 94–115.

Rosen, L. D. 2011. "Teaching the iGeneration." *Educational Leadership*, 68 (5), 10–15.

Roskos, K. A., P. O. Tabors, and L. A. Lenhart. 2009. *Oral Language and Early Literacy in Preschool: Talking, Reading, and Writing.* Newark, DE: International Reading Association.

Saunders, W. G., and G. O'Brien. 2006. "Oral Language." In *Educating English Language Learners: A Synthesis of Research Evidence*, edited by F. Genesee, K. Lindholm-Leary, B. Saunders, and D. Christian, 14–48. New York: Cambridge University Press.

Schleppegrell, M., and O'Halloran, C. 2011. "Teaching Academic Language in L2 Secondary Settings." *Annual Review of Applied Linguistics* 31, 3–18.

Shafer Willner, L. 2013. *Proficiency Level Descriptors for English Language Proficiency Standards.* Washington DC: Council of Chief State School Officers.

Shanahan, T., and C. Shanahan. 2008. "Teaching Disciplinary Literacy to Adolescents: Rethinking Content-Area Literacy." *Harvard Educational Review* 78: 40–59.

Short, D. J., and B. A. Boyson. 2012. "Helping Newcomer Students Succeed in Secondary Schools and Beyond." Washington, DC: Center for Applied Linguistics. https://www.carnegie.org/media/filer_public/ff/fd/fffda48e-4211-44c5-b4ef -86e8b50929d6/ccny_report_2012_helping.pdf.

Sibold, C. 2011. "Building English Language Learners' Academic Vocabulary: Strategies and Tips." *Multicultural Education* 18: 24–28.

Singer, T. W. 2014. *Opening Doors to Equity: A Practical Guide to Observation-Based Professional Learning.* Thousand Oaks, CA: Corwin.

Slavin, R. E. 1995. *Cooperative Learning: Theory, Research, and Practice,* Second edition. Boston: Allyn & Bacon.

Soto, I. 2014. *Moving from Spoken to Written Language with ELLs.* Thousand Oaks, CA: Corwin.

Sousa, D. 2011. *How the Brain Learns,* Fourth edition. Thousand Oaks, CA: Corwin.

Staehr Fenner, D., and S. Snyder. 2014. "Socratic Circles and the Common Core: An Introduction (Part I)." http://www.colorincolorado.org/blog/socratic-circles -and-common-core-introduction-part-i.

Stock, P. L., T. Schillinger, and A. Stock. 2014. *Entering the Conversations: Practicing Literacy in the Disciplines.* Urbana, IL: National Council of Teachers of English.

Temple, C. A., D. Ogle, A. N. Crawford, and P. Freppon. 2013. *All Children Read: Teaching for Literacy in Today's Diverse Classrooms*, Fourth edition. Upper Saddle River, NJ: Pearson.

TESOL. 2018. *The 6 Principles for Exemplary Teaching of English Learners Grades K–12.* Alexandria, VA: TESOL International Association.

Thorpe, H. 2017. *The Newcomers: Finding Refuge, Friendship, and Hope in an American Classroom.* New York: Scribner.

Trelease, J. 2013. *The Read-Aloud Handbook.* 7th ed. New York: Penguin.

Tung, R. 2013. "Innovations in Educational Equity for English Language Learners." (Special issue: English Language Learners: Shifting to an Asset-Based Paradigm.) *Voices in Urban Education,* 2–5. http://vue.annenberginstitute.org/sites/default/files/issuePDF/VUE37.pdf

Valdés, G., Poza, L., and Brooks, M. D. 2015. "Language Acquisition in Bilingual Education." In *The Handbook of Bilingual and Multilingual Education*, edited by W. E. Wright, S. Boun, and O. García, 56–74. Malden, MA: Wiley-Blackwell.

Velasco, P., and O. García. 2014. "Translanguaging and the Writing of Bilingual Learners." *Bilingual Research Journal* 37: 6–23.

Vygotsky, L. 1978. *Mind in Society.* Cambridge, UK: Cambridge University Press.

Walqui, A. 2006. "Scaffolding Instruction for English Language Learners: A Conceptual Framework." *International Journal of Bilingual Education and Bilingualism* 9: 159–180.

Walqui, A., and Heritage, M. 2012. *Instruction for Diverse Groups of English Language Learners.* Paper presented at the Understanding Language Conference, Stanford, CA. http://ell.stanford.edu/papers.

Walqui, A., and L. van Lier. 2010. *Scaffolding the Academic Success of Adolescent English Language Learners: A Pedagogy of Promise.* San Francisco: Wested.

Washor, E., and C. Mojkowski. 2013. *Leaving to Learn: How Out-of-School Learning Increases Student Engagement and Reduces Dropout Rates.* Portsmouth, NH: Heinemann.

WIDA. 2012. "English Language Proficiency Standards." www.wida.us.

Yahya, N., and K. Huie. 2002. "Reaching English Language Learners Through Cooperative Learning." *The Internet TESL Journal* 8 (3). http://iteslj.org/Articles/Yahya-Cooperative.html.

Yenawine, P. 2013. *Visual Thinking Strategies: Using Art to Deepen Learning Across School Disciplines.* Cambridge, MA: Harvard Education Press.

Zacarian, D., and J. Haynes. 2012. *The Essential Guide for Educating Beginning English Learners*. Thousand Oaks, CA: Corwin.

Zike, D. 1992. *Big Book of Books*. San Antonio, TX: Dinah-Might Adventures.

———. 2012. *Dinah Zike's Envelope Graphic Organizers: Using Repurposed Envelopes for Projects, Study Guides, and Daily Work*. San Antonio, TX: Dinah-Might Adventures.

Zwiers, J. 2014. *Building Academic Language: Meeting Common Core Standards Across Disciplines: Grades 5–12*, Second edition. San Francisco: Jossey Bass

———. 2018. "Fortifying Speaking & Listening Skills." http://jeffzwiers.org/fortifying -speaking.